Leadership from the Ground Up

LEADERSHIP
FROM THE GROUND UP

ANGELA L. WALKER FRANKLIN, PH.D.

bpc

Leadership from the Ground Up is published by Business Publications Corporation Inc., an Iowa corporation.

Copyright © 2024 by Angela L. Walker Franklin, Ph.D.

Reproduction or other use, in whole or in part, of the contents without permission of the publisher is strictly prohibited.

ISBN: 978-1-950790-14-2
Library of Congress Control Number: 2024915187
Business Publications Corporation Inc., Des Moines, IA

Business Publications Corporation Inc.
The Plaza
300 Walnut Street, Suite 5
Des Moines, Iowa 50309
(515) 288-3336

This book is dedicated to all the women who have ever doubted their ability to lead.

CONTENTS

Photo Section Begins on Page 62

ACKNOWLEDGMENTS | i

PREFACE | 1
Daring to Dream Big

CHAPTER 1 | 7
An Unusual Start: A Most Public Offer

CHAPTER 2 | 13
Servant Leadership: The Principles I Brought to the Task

CHAPTER 3 | 23
The First Week: Surprises and Lessons Learned

CHAPTER 4 | 29
The First Hundred Days: A Call to Action

CHAPTER 5 | 35
The Battle Begins: The Honeymoon Ends

CHAPTER 6 | 43
Fresh Ideas and Positive Thinking: Key Leadership Transitions

CHAPTER 7 | 49
The Executive Leadership Team: Calling Out the Elephant in the Room

CHAPTER 8 | 55
Engaging the Campus Community: Creating an Inclusive Culture

CHAPTER 9 | 77
Lessons in Leadership: How Do You Build Trust with Strangers?

CHAPTER 10 | 85
The Vital Dynamic: Confrontation, Validation, and the Board of Trustees

CHAPTER 11 | 93
An Entirely New Campus: Mobilizing Our Community

CHAPTER 12 | 101
Leadership from the Ground Up: Working as a Team

CHAPTER 13 | 105
Living the Double Standard: Stereotypes, Judgments, and First Impressions

CHAPTER 14 | 109
World Conditions and Respect for Everyone: Personal and Organizational Transitions

EPILOGUE | 113
Living the Dream

APPENDIX 1 | 115
2011 Inaugural Address

APPENDIX 2 | 125
Executive Leadership Team Covenant

ACKNOWLEDGMENTS

I would not be where I am today if not for the love and support of so many. My parents, Leola and H.W. Walker, were relentless in their efforts to make sure I was well prepared for a challenging world that might not accept me for who I am. I was filled with words of encouragement and clear expectations about what high academic achievement would provide to me. My first understanding of how to push forward, defy the odds, and prove people wrong in their perceptions of me came from them. Thank you, Mom and Dad. I know you are watching from above.

My husband gets the credit for being the steady hand of quiet support … never doubting, always there, cheering me on. Thank you, Thad, for being my rock, my strong shoulder of support, with your encouraging "you've got this, go for it."

Several mentors have provided guidance and affirmation of my ability to lead. Thank you, Dr. Louis Sullivan, for reminding me not to settle for playing second fiddle but instead to go where I'm wanted. And Dr. George Keller, who first told me to step out of my comfort zone and aim high.

To my editor, Holly Carver, I thank you for the sage advice and the affirmation that my message resonates with a broader audience than I may have imagined.

PREFACE

DARING TO DREAM BIG

This story begins with a bold decision by a university's board of trustees to hire a new leader who came with a history of achieving success in spite of many obstacles. I described myself in an earlier memoir as someone who sincerely believed that she was a most unlikely choice. The reality of this belief comes from being a tough-skinned African American woman who dared to achieve. The belief comes from real-life experiences in which my legitimacy and my credentials were questioned. The belief comes from the blatant disregard of my efforts to go over and above the basic level of expectations and present myself as more than qualified.

In that memoir, *An Unconventional Journey ... An Unlikely Choice*, I wrote about my doubts and trepidations as I pursued a college presidency. I outlined the ways that my small-town upbringing in the segregated South shaped my style and philosophy of leadership and led me to a career in higher education. I wrote about how, drawing upon my Ph.D. in clinical psychology, I held academic and administrative positions at Atlanta's Morehouse School of Medicine before becoming provost and executive vice president at Meharry Medical College in Nashville. The book ended when I accepted the opportunity to serve as president of Des Moines University Medicine and Health Sciences.

What happened after I arrived in 2011 is a case study in leadership with all the challenges involved in assessing and restructuring an organization that had potential for greatness while trying to reinvigorate a talented group of colleagues to step out of their comfort zones and imagine a future that they might have seen as impossible. "Dreaming big" was just a catchphrase to some and a nice rallying cry that really didn't mean much to the campus population in those early years. However, I always felt that I was brought to Des Moines University for a reason and that I had a calling to serve an organization that had the potential to be much more than it had been. The idea that the university was a best-kept secret often bothered me; I thought that was too shortsighted and too comfortable. To be something more meant taking a bold look at what was possible, then stepping up to push forward to achieve it.

For those who wondered about the rest of the story after reading my memoir, I will now share what happened after I arrived, from the honeymoon phase to the tumult of storms and battles to the fine organization that we now have—an organization that has endured many challenges and has overcome them. Those of you coming to my story for the first time will, I hope, find inspiration and courage and a fresh point of view that will help you overcome your own challenges. I will describe the twists and turns in the journey that I took to become a college president, as well as the journey that taught me to navigate the challenges of being the first, of being the change agent, and of being the transformative leader of an organization that today thrives as a national leader in medical education.

Theories of leadership effectiveness abound. Basic principles, novel ideas, and creative iterations fill bookstores, webinars, and executive conferences around the world. As a leader in higher education, I have read many of them, often finding pearls of wisdom and numerous affirmations of what has worked for me.

I believe that I offer a unique perspective on leadership here, one unique to the traditional career paths of college presidents. I will share some of my basic principles of leadership as they apply to my current environment. But I will go one step further and provide the answer to the question, "How did you mobilize an organization to realize big, audacious, transformative goals?" My approach has allowed Des Moines University both to achieve success and to thrive against the odds. I believe something special has evolved here, and this will be my opportunity to tell you about it and, I hope, to inspire you to achieve your own successes.

Frankly, we all have been surprised at just how great an impact that decision to hire me has had on the future trajectory of Des Moines University. I was surprised when they invited me to become their new president. And they were surprised when I accepted their invitation. Twelve years later, as I write this, I can look back and see the lessons learned, the goals achieved, and the dreams realized as we move to an entirely new campus, built on eighty-eight acres of farmland, to create an innovative health sciences university literally from the ground up!

So, I may have thought that I was a most unlikely choice in 2011. Yet now, I firmly believe that I was the right choice at the right time to transform this organization to go beyond any previous expectations. "Dreaming big" was not only a rallying cry. It has also become our reality.

Leadership from the Ground Up

CHAPTER 1

AN UNUSUAL START: A MOST PUBLIC OFFER

The interview process for senior-level administrators in higher education is fairly standard across most organizations, especially if managed by external search and consulting firms. The process was quite familiar to me as I enthusiastically planned my on-campus visit to Des Moines University after being selected as a presidential finalist shortly after my airport interview in September 2010.

I came back to Des Moines in late October 2010 for my visit with the board of trustees. At the time, I was aware that I was one of three finalists, and when I arrived in town, I soon learned that my competition was, one, the current interim president and, two, a former mayor of a suburban city in the metropolitan area. I was perplexed by this lineup. Needless to say, I assumed that the board would follow the past model and either hire another politician as the university's fifteenth president or simply stay with the status quo: a long-term administrator who had served as the interim president for several months. Frankly, I wondered why I was still being courted.

My visit to Des Moines was amazing. Everyone on campus and in the community really rolled out the red carpet. I had the usual expected interviews with groups as well as an all-campus presentation. The finale, however, was an afternoon "community reception" that had not been well defined. When my husband, Thad, and I were picked up at the Savery Hotel by a member of the development staff, Duane Murray, I asked where we were going for this reception. He responded, "Out to West Des Moines."

We were actually going to his own private residence, which confused me, but we waited intently as we navigated the neighborhood streets to his home in West Des Moines. As we parked in his driveway, I noticed cars lining the street, never imagining that the crowd had already piled into his lovely home. Smiling and greeting me at the door was Willie Stevenson Glanton, a board of trustees member and a well-respected leader of the African American community. Now I was really confused.

To our surprise, the home was packed with many well-wishers, most of whom were African American and other people of color. I will never forget the smiles on their faces and their warm greetings. When I reminded them all that I was simply a candidate, not the new president, the response I got back was simply stated: "We know, but we are all praying for you and want you to know that if you are selected to be the next president of DMU, you will not be here alone. There will be a community of people of color cheering you on in support of this noteworthy appointment." I still get chills when I remember that afternoon. There were ministers of churches, physicians, educators, business leaders, and others who simply wanted to say, "Welcome! And we are proud to know that you have a shot at getting this job."

The ride back to the hotel was quiet, yet Thad and I could not hold back the pure excitement and joy we felt as we acknowledged the most sincere and genuine act of kindness we had ever experienced. Now I had an even greater desire to join this community—if only I were selected. The idea of becoming the fifteenth president of Des Moines University now seemed plausible, and my excitement was building.

After that visit, I waited. I remember being frustrated at Thanksgiving by not hearing anything. I remained quiet, albeit sullen, as I faced the reality of what was happening. Why string me along? Not again! This began to feel very much like a previous presidential search experience. I began second-guessing everything and doubting that I was really a serious candidate.

I now know that the trustees were struggling with their own challenges within the board. And they were anxious about making such a bold decision, about how it would be received by the campus and the community. A few weeks later, I was invited back for a second on-campus visit. I came to know that the trustees felt this was such a monumental decision for the university that they needed to make sure the entire board fully endorsed their decision. So, I returned alone to meet with the full board on December 4, 2010. It was a cold, dreary, and snowy day. I again made plans to stay one night at the Savery Hotel, but this time I was not so sure about what was going on. I remember being encouraged by the search firm's consultant, who simply said, "Just go and see. No harm in that."

When I arrived on campus that afternoon, I was placed in an empty office down the hall from the boardroom and told that I would be called in when they were ready for me. Apparently, the other two candidates were also to be seen by the entire board.

It was about 2:30 in the afternoon on that Saturday when they called me in. As I walked into the boardroom, about twenty-five faces all smiled at me. I was told to sit down at the end of the table, and then Chairman Jim Grekin began asking questions, some of the same questions I had been asked so many times before. A few other board members also asked questions, which I believe I answered quite well. After about forty-five minutes of questioning, Dr. Grekin said I could go and thanked me for my time. It felt like another blow. I wondered, "Why bring me back here again and not just tell me once and for all if you want me to be your president or not?" I was shouting to myself, "So just what in the world are you doing? Do you want me or not? What is this game you're playing?"

Becky Lade, the director of human resources, drove me back to the Savery. I asked her sincerely, "What can I expect now?" She answered, "I have no idea." She added, "The chairman of the board, Dr. Grekin, has taken over the process, and neither the search firm's consultant nor the committee has any idea at this point what they may do." Additionally, "They have all your contact numbers, and my guess is that he will likely call you when any decision is made." Bummer!

I entered the hotel and rode the elevator up to my room, frustrated and disconcerted. I remember getting to my room and staring out the window at the Iowa State Capitol with its dirty remnants of a recent snowfall and thinking, "So, who would want to live here anyway?!"

Within a few minutes of that thought, my cell phone rang with a number I did not recognize. It wasn't a Tennessee number or an Iowa number, so I answered with a gruff, "Hello, who is this?" To my surprise, the voice that answered belonged to Dr. Jim Grekin. He said, "Dr. Franklin, this is Jim Grekin. Are you sitting down?" I said, "Oh, yes, I can sit down." He then said, "We, the members of the Des Moines University board of trustees, would like to offer you the position of president and CEO of Des Moines University." Silence. I could not believe what I was hearing. My next comment was, "So, where are you? I just left the campus a few minutes ago." He said, "Yes, we are all still here in the boardroom, and we just voted with a unanimous decision to offer you the role."

I must admit that I was stunned. I couldn't process quickly enough what was happening. Dr. Grekin then yelled, "Hey, folks, she doesn't believe we are all still here! Can you make some noise so she knows I'm telling the truth and we are all here and excited about this decision?" I could then hear cheering and clapping in the background. The next thing he said was, "Well, I haven't heard a yes yet."

The next thing that came out of my mouth was, "Well, will I get a contract? I need to know what I'm saying yes to." He said, "Well, we are sending Steve Morain down to the Savery in a few minutes to bring you an offer letter." I then said, "Yes, I will accept contingent upon negotiating reasonable terms in a contract that I look forward to seeing." He said, "We are happy to hear that, and, by the way, can you join me at our holiday party?" Duh?! Inviting me to the holiday party was shocking, but what do you do? You say, "Well, of course I will!"

But I had many more questions. A holiday party? For real? If I come to this, what will people know? I'm honored to be invited, but how will this play out? My other concern was whether the interim president, who was also a candidate, would be there. I was told yes, he would be there, but he had already been told that I had been offered the job and he was excited to meet me. This seemed really strange, but I accepted it at face value. The next strange thing was the fact that I had just happened to bring a party dress with appropriate bling. Who knew?

The next few minutes after I hung up with Dr. Grekin, I continued to sit on the edge of the bed, literally shaking with excitement. Then I called Thad. "Guess what? They offered me the job." "How much?" "I don't know. They are bringing a letter to me soon, but I also agreed to go to their holiday party." Thad's response: "What the hell!?"

Steve Morain, a board of trustees member, arrived with the letter of appointment, a simple three-page document that began with a statement offering me the job, and we met in a restaurant at the Savery. I read it quickly, then noticed a strange statement about not campaigning or involving myself in political campaigns. In their haste, they had simply reworked the letter of appointment of the previous president, former Iowa Governor Terry Branstad, which had language regarding politics. When I pointed this out, Steve simply said, "Oh no, we can take that out." I accepted the letter and vowed to get back to them with a decision as soon as I got home and had an opportunity to talk with my legal counsel.

The holiday party, however, was quite the spectacle. I didn't realize as I walked into the Des Lux Hotel atrium that I would be the only person of color. People stopped and stared, and it was clear that the word was already out that I had been offered the position. The vice president for development, Sue Huppert, approached me first and welcomed me, offering to take my coat and getting me something to drink. It was an awkward start to a strange evening as I tried my best to be a wallflower and blend into the background.

Steve Dengel came over to introduce himself; he was the interim president who had not been selected. He congratulated me on getting the job. Then Chairman Jim Grekin came over to welcome me, announcing that he wanted to introduce me to the people gathered. I was shocked and reminded him that I had not formally accepted the role and that this was contingent upon us coming to terms on a contract. He did not seem to care and instead proceeded to the stage, asking people to gather around. After he introduced me as the new president and CEO of Des Moines University, he handed me the microphone to say a few words. I thanked him for the opportunity to meet everyone and wished them all happy holidays.

Board member Hal Hatchett offered to take me back to the hotel, and I ended the evening staring out the window of the hotel, looking at the state Capitol. Now, it no longer looked cold and dreary. It was beautiful, and I was excited to say, with a laugh and a giggle, "What in the world just happened here?"

CHAPTER 2

SERVANT LEADERSHIP: THE PRINCIPLES I BROUGHT TO THE TASK

On March 1, 2011, when I came to Des Moines University to begin this journey, I carried twelve hard-earned, well-considered principles with me, principles that reflected my style of leadership and that would form the foundation of the mission before me.

The theory of servant leadership, a phrase coined by Robert Greenleaf in "The Servant as Leader," an essay he published in 1970, is the backdrop for my style of leadership, which begins with first having the right attitude. It is never about the individual but always about the organization. The more the leader has a glass-half-full attitude, the more likely it is that this positive attitude will spread.

The principles of servant leadership have spiritual ties, and this opportunity strengthened my resolve to lead with the basic understanding that I was chosen to serve, not to be served. I therefore came to Des Moines University with the clear understanding that I had a calling to serve—to fulfill my purpose and provide leadership to an organization that chose ME!

I did not take the board's decision lightly; I appreciated the bold decision that the trustees had made to select someone who may have been perceived to be different from the usual and customary candidate. Being the first woman and the first person of color to lead the second-oldest osteopathic medical college in the United States was a Big Deal. The trustees understood the magnitude of their decision; although they were a bit nervous about how I would be received and accepted, they were strong in their convictions that they had chosen the right person to lead. I, too, had my doubts and worries, yet I stepped out on faith, leaving my family and support structure behind in Nashville initially because I truly felt that I was called to serve. I was committed to do my best because there was no room for error or failure.

These twelve basic principles came along with me to Des Moines University. I still hold them close as I continue to evolve in my leadership journey. These principles have been put to the test repeatedly. Whereas all twelve remain important to me, I believe that mutual respect, honesty and truthfulness, the ability to listen, and team spirit best define the success I have achieved in sustaining my leadership effectiveness over the years.

ONE: HAVE THE RIGHT ATTITUDE

There is nothing more important than your outlook and personal style. I believe effective leaders need to begin with the correct mindset, which includes a sincere desire and willingness to serve others. It is a conscious decision to step into a challenging role with a clear focus. Without the right mindset, leaders will not be able to ensure that group goals are met. Instead, they can appear to be acting for personal gain. The worst mistake leaders can make is to take on the role with the attitude that they have arrived and that it is all about them.

TWO: BE AN ADVOCATE FOR MUTUAL RESPECT

An essential ingredient in leadership is a genuine wish to value people as people and to treat them the way you would want to be treated. There have been some very interesting twists on this statement that raise the question: Can you know someone well enough to know exactly how they would want to be treated? Believe it or not, there has been a challenge to the Golden Rule. What is fascinating about this is that those who choose to raise this question seem to be forgetting a basic principle, which is simply mutual respect. Who would *not* want to be treated with kindness and respect? Plain and simple, we should all value this basic principle.

I do not need to know much more about a person other than the fact that he or she is human and deserves respect. On the other hand, there may be value in acknowledging that we all come from different cultures and experiences, and it is important to reach people where they are. But I would say that it is likely impossible to really *know* everyone well enough to know exactly how they would want to be treated. The basic premise of the Golden Rule focuses on the basics of respect, compassion, and kindness. It does not matter if I know your culture or ethnicity. There simply is a universal standard of treating people with kindness. We all can do that regardless of who we are and where we come from.

THREE: LISTEN EFFECTIVELY

Psychologists are trained to be good listeners. There is a skill involved, but it is also a simple thing to do. Communication is a two-way process, and it is so important for a leader to learn how to shut up and listen. Stephen Covey says, "Seek first to understand, then seek to be understood." This reflects the epitome of effective listening. Everyone is entitled to his or her own opinion, and it is so important to value the opinions of all. An often-used phrase states that you should allow everyone to have a voice, which simply means that it is important to give everyone an opportunity to be heard. Ineffective listening undermines self-esteem, self-confidence, and creativity. Think of the impact of empowering someone who has a great idea to feel as if their opinion is valued and heard. It also is most important to acknowledge that hearing and listening are not synonymous. The worst mistake you can make as a leader is to sit quietly to hear people speak, then, in the very next breath, run over them with your own ideas without acknowledging that you heard or valued anything that they said.

FOUR: EMBRACE HONESTY AND TRUTHFULNESS

I pride myself on being an authentic person, flaunting no frills, being consistent, and calling it as I see it. Being trustworthy is essential to maintaining credibility in a leadership role. Your word is everything—and believe me, there are so many times that your words are misconstrued or misinterpreted that it is important to remain genuine and consistent. I find myself having to correct misrepresentations of things that I say. If I am honest and consistent in my message, then it is easy to clear up misinterpretations. However, if my story keeps changing and I convey different messages depending on the circumstances, then it is more difficult to explain misinterpretations. Being authentic allows me to be real.

As for honesty and truthfulness, your word is your word. It is entirely possible to be truthful and compassionate at the same time. It is never right, however, to malign someone and make hurtful statements. We gain nothing from being brutally honest when we mean only to hurt. Yet beginning with honesty allows us to be perceived as trustworthy.

FIVE: EXPECT CONFLICT

I wish the world were perfect! I wish all people were perfect, but we are not. We are all flawed, and we all have our own little quirks. The richness of interactions with others comes from the diverse opinions that we all bring to the table. We are bound to have differing opinions, which leads to conflict. I expect it and plan for it. In any work or family situation, conflict is inevitable and a constant factor in human interactions. An effective leader expects conflict and is able to manage it in a productive manner. This is never easy, but leaders must make concerted efforts to set expectations and build a culture of openness. When conflicts arrive, it is important to get the issues on the table for all to see and to deal with them in a timely manner, because prolonging conflict only makes matters worse.

Conflict is the most difficult of the principles to manage because of its emotionality. Many times, conflicts occur because people are not able to differentiate between task-related conflict and their personal investment in a given situation. It is so important to separate the two. When conflicts become personalized, it is more difficult to separate feelings from facts. The facts can be more easily addressed if the feelings are acknowledged and put into proper perspective. Do I expect to get along with everyone all the time? Do I expect everyone to agree with the decisions I make? No! Happiness, satisfaction, pleasure, and contentment should be by-products of the goodwill that comes from working together to manage conflict in a civil, collegial manner by staying focused on the facts and finding common ground.

SIX: BE PROACTIVE

Early in my tenure as a faculty member, I was often in the position of either volunteering to serve on committees or leading a particular work group or project. I was always eager to learn and looked at every new opportunity as résumé building. Knowledge is power, and the more you engage, the more you learn. Stepping up to the plate to lead allows you to be validated. Inserting yourself into the mix gives you visibility and credibility. When all else fails, ask for the opportunity!

This is similar to the impressions shared in Sheryl Sandberg's book *Lean In: Women, Work, and the Will to Lead*. Too many times, women, in particular, sit on their hands and wait for someone else to take the lead. I remember once being told that I should not always volunteer to take the minutes in meetings since it was perceived to be expected of the women in the group. I often found myself being the only female in several meetings early on in my career. I did not mind taking the minutes and never thought of it as demeaning or stereotypical. What it gave me, eventually, was an opportunity to lead. For she who takes the minutes controls the history! As the recorder of the action steps, I soon became the go-to person who knew how to set the next agenda because I had the details from the previous meeting. Being proactive and stepping up to the plate can be empowering. Don't underestimate the power of small steps!

SEVEN: MAINTAIN YOUR COMMITMENT

As I struggled with purpose along my journey, I found myself questioning my level of commitment. I often asked myself why I was still at the Morehouse School of Medicine after twenty years. Clearly, I was committed to the mission of the school but even more committed to the students I served. I often joked with them that I made a personal commitment to help them achieve their goals when I introduced them at first-year orientation. Somehow, my commitment extended to seeing them cross the stage at graduation so that I could be the first to call them by their new title. That commitment may have been why I stayed there so long. My engagement was such that as soon as I brought a new class of students in, I felt committed to seeing them march across the stage.

It was difficult to shift my thinking and allow myself to let go of that very restricted and limiting approach. Yes, I maintained my commitment to aid and assist future health professionals to reach their goals, but I realized I did not necessarily have to do so only at this one institution.

That commitment, however, was what kept me going during challenging times. I was in it for all the right reasons, and getting caught up in the mission of the school was easy. It was not about me, and it was not just about giving lip service. It is so important to express your commitment through your thoughts and actions. Ask yourself this: Are you really in it for the right reasons?

EIGHT: TAKE RISKS

One trait of a great leader is an ability to take risks. If you are risk-averse, beware. It is so important to be able to step outside the box and think innovatively. Flexibility of thought and action is a must. A leader must be able to know when it's time to try a new approach or implement a new policy. Being stuck in a rut with comfort as the status quo never advances an agenda. Be a student of your own profession. Learn, be innovative, do your homework, and get a grasp on what the best practices are. No one wants a stagnant leader. There is excitement in innovation that pushes your organization forward.

NINE: ACKNOWLEDGE AUTHORITY AND ADHERE TO POLICIES

Everyone has a boss, and everyone has to answer to someone. I answer first to a spiritual power, and I get my faith from this most exalted leader. However, it is equally important to show respect and be accountable to those in authority even when you do not believe they have earned your respect. Your boss is your boss until you choose to be somewhere else. In the same vein, it is important to adhere to the policies of your organization, staying aligned with its goals and procedures until you perceive a need for change.

There are some environments where written policies, which were established in the past, are ignored, and everyone chooses instead to follow the practices and guidelines that have evolved over time. In this case you, as the leader, have demonstrated that there are no policies. A leader should acknowledge when there is a need to create policies when none exist, change policies that no longer work, and abide by those that exist. Otherwise, the integrity of an organization is undermined.

TEN: ENCOURAGE TEAM SPIRIT

It is so important to build trust within an organization. This is another one of those principles that takes quite a bit of time to fulfill. It is important to set clear expectations and let people do their jobs. It is also important to create an environment where people matter—to foster a sense of team spirit and camaraderie. I love the idea of the "warm fuzzy," and a simple acknowledgment of thanks is so easy to do. People want to feel that they are valued members of a team. Saying "thank you for all that you do" goes a long way toward building morale and fostering a sense of team spirit.

ELEVEN: TAKE MINOR PROBLEMS LIGHTLY

The phrase "don't sweat the small stuff" expresses the desire to avoid getting bogged down in minutiae. There are conflicts and challenges in any work environment, but it is crucial to concentrate on what is most important, decide whether the battle is worth fighting, and remain cool, calm, and collected. There will be days when you feel that everything is broken. I sometimes talk of the fires that are blazing all around me on days when I cannot seem to get anything done. An unexpected situation always appears out of nowhere.

I typically do not let myself get too excited—instead, I choose not to wear my feelings on my sleeve. This is a skill that you can learn if it is not instinctive to you. The best leader during challenging times is someone who can calmly focus, think clearly and strategically, and directly address problems. Keeping emotions at bay is also important. Learn to create a mental parking lot to hold the things that you cannot understand or explain and leave them there. Then go home and get ready to fight another day. There are no perfect environments and no perfect people. The institutions we serve will still have challenges when we leave, and we will never be able to make them perfect. Striving for perfection is fine, but it is more important to know how to celebrate the small successes that help move an organization forward.

TWELVE: TAKE CARE OF YOURSELF

My training in psychology allows me to remain focused on ensuring that I maintain my own sanity in a sometimes-insane world. I am a major proponent of prevention and wellness, and working in an institution that has wellness as a core value is an ever-greater testament to the fact that I am in the right place. We all know the basic rules of living a healthy lifestyle, but many of us still struggle to do the right thing.

I believe there are psychological and personality variables that help define who can succeed in taking a disciplined approach to health and wellness. Eat right, exercise, do what the doctor says—these seem simple enough, but we often do not take our own advice. It is important to reduce stress in our lives as best we can, but it is even more important to recognize when things are out of control and when we need help. It is so important to seek help early. Taking good care of yourself and being a bit selfish when it comes to that will allow you to be available to help others. The serenity prayer sums it up nicely: "God, grant me the serenity to accept the things I cannot change, courage to change the things I can, and wisdom to know the difference."

Come along with me as I share the rest of the story of how these twelve principles were challenged and how I persevered, plowing through the hard times and coming out on the other side with an organization that has been transformed.

CHAPTER 3

THE FIRST WEEK: SURPRISES AND LESSONS LEARNED

Becoming the first! Becoming the first woman and the first person of color to serve as president and CEO of Des Moines University was a major milestone. This journey to the college presidency was, yes, unconventional, and at first I actually believed that I was the most unlikely choice for this particular role. Perhaps my self-doubt got in the way, in spite of the fact that I knew I was well prepared for this role, having spent years working in higher ed in various capacities. The irony is that no matter how well prepared we are, women, in general, typically sell themselves short; we often think that we need to know more and do more to be accepted as being good enough.

The American Council on Education conducts its American College President Study approximately every five years. Over a thousand presidents responded to the 2022 survey and, as was seen in earlier iterations, college presidents remained older, white, and male. Men still outnumbered women two to one in the presidency. Presidents of color accounted for a little over one out of four presidents. And women of color accounted for a little more than one out of every ten presidents.

When I was offered the job of being the fifteenth president of Des Moines University, my first reaction was, "Are you kidding me?" Trying to set my self-doubt aside, I tried to convince myself that I was indeed prepared, that I was indeed the right person for the job, that I could believe the trustees when they said they were looking for someone just like me. My academic background in medical education set me apart from the other finalists, and the board had clearly pursued me, reminding me of a phrase often shared with me by my mentor, Dr. Louis W. Sullivan: "Go where you are wanted."

We negotiated a start date of March 1, 2011. I decided I would come alone because, frankly, I wasn't sure if relocating my entire family was the right thing to do. It seemed too risky. The doubt remained.

Because my husband had not shared any details of my aspirations with his bosses, we had decided not to pursue the idea that he might relocate until it was clear that he needed to move. Getting the offer to go to Des Moines didn't change our approach, since we assumed that with one son still in high school and a relatively slow real estate market, our family would remain in Nashville for at least a year. This would give me time to see whether Des Moines was a good fit.

We had addressed the question of moving our youngest son for his senior year of high school, and Jordan was very open to spending his senior year in Iowa. "Frankly," he said, "I welcome the opportunity to have my own high school." Middle son Grant had already started college at Western Kentucky University, and Wesley had graduated from Furman University and moved with us to Nashville, where he was completing his master's degree and looking to begin his career.

Jordan decided he would join me at the end of the academic year to attend Valley High School for his senior year. It happened to be in West Des Moines, and therefore we needed to live in West Des Moines. Grant decided he would transfer from Western Kentucky to Drake University, where he could walk on to the football team, which had been his dream. I was surprised that Des Moines University had no president's residence—no president in recent years had needed a home—so the question of where I would live became an issue. In a series of visits to Des Moines, I located an empty house for sale in Glen Oaks, a gated community, which Thad thought would be safer for me living alone. I rented it with the thought that we would later purchase it.

On February 27, 2011, Thad and I packed up the truck and a U-Haul trailer with a bed frame, an old sofa, a few boxes of pots and pans, and my clothes and set out to drive to Des Moines. Des Moines University would provide a car, and the board would reimburse me for the monthly expense of renting this empty house. When we arrived in the middle of a blizzard, I thought, "What the hell have I done?"

My first day on the job coincided with the annual president's reception, where community leaders came to hear the president give a state-of-the-union address. The previous president, Terry Branstad, who had by then been again elected governor of Iowa, was there to introduce me. I was handed a script with talking points of recent accomplishments that I was determined to deliver on my own, whether they made sense to me or not.

This first reception was crowded. Having no point of reference, I thought it was a nice gathering of about a hundred campus and community members. Standing out in the crowd, however, were my sisters from Delta Sigma Theta sorority. It was a warm welcome from all and a nice treat to have my sorors wish me well at the start of my journey. My journey as president and CEO of Des Moines University began with grand fanfare!

On my second day on the job, I flew to Sarasota to join the board of trustees for its annual retreat. This was a truly eye-opening experience for me as I met Dr. Ellen Chaffee, a consultant from the Association of Governing Boards of Universities and Colleges, whom board leadership had hired to assist with orienting the new president and to conduct a board governance retreat for the first time.

To my surprise, the entire administrative team also flew to Sarasota, although they spent most of their time outside of the board meeting, not inside. The optics concerned me. For a tuition-dependent institution, how did it look to have the entire board of trustees, support staff, and key administrators who formed the president's cabinet traveling to Florida for a four-day stay with all the amenities at a major beach resort?

I understood that my role at the retreat was to sit and observe. Dr. Chaffee was charged with doing a presentation on best practices in board governance and directing the trustees toward the most efficient policies and procedures. Chairman Jim Grekin was not necessarily open to these ideas, and my first observation of this came when Dr. Chaffee's attempts to talk about best practices were often met with sneers and eye rolls. The more she talked, the less the board chair wanted to listen. I felt a deep sense of worry. What had I gotten myself into?

This was a deer-in-the-headlights moment for me as I sat quietly, listening to a wonderful presentation interrupted by constant challenges to ideas that, to me, seemed quite basic. At our first break, when I spoke with Dr. Chaffee, she expressed her concern with a look that I interpreted to mean, "Oh my, I'm so sorry you will have to deal with this board."

The next surprise of the retreat came when I asked what happened to the cabinet members while the board was meeting. Chairman Grekin essentially said, "Oh, they are enjoying the resort. They love coming down here to enjoy the facilities."

The cabinet members were sitting on the sidelines as if unsure of how or whether to engage with me. So I invited them out to dinner—something I learned had never happened before. Because I thought it important to begin building rapport with them, I asked Linda Kading, the board secretary, to arrange an evening for us all to have dinner together. The mere suggestion of an outing with the president seemed to be a foreign concept.

That trip down the road to a seafood joint was revealing. My best efforts to connect were met with resistance because the cabinet members typically considered any engagement with the president to be a burden, not something they would ever want to do. When we all piled into a minivan to ride about a mile down the road to have dinner, the nervous chatter on the drive there and back gave me pause. It took a bold statement from the mischievous dean of the College of Podiatric Medicine and Surgery, Tim Yoho, to capture the moment when he joked, "We've never been taken to dinner by the president. The president normally hangs with the board, and we just do our own thing."

Another surprise, another lesson learned: cabinets and presidents did not mix! I was determined to change that!

At the end of the retreat, I was given a charge by the board. I was asked to do a hundred-day assessment and report my findings at the May board meeting. When I asked for more specifics, some board members described this as an audit, something that an accreditation team would come in to perform. They indicated that they didn't know what they didn't know, and they thought that this assessment would be useful for me as the new president and would also serve to better inform them of the health of the organization. They particularly asked me to assess the culture of the place.

I left Sarasota having learned that members of the president's cabinet also did not think it wise for them to be there; they were also concerned about the message it sent to the larger campus community. And they felt that the trip was a waste of time since they spent most of the time doing their own work, not engaging with the board.

Quietly, I vowed to eliminate the retreat. I added it to my list of things that just didn't feel right, but I knew it would take time to make the adjustment. There were just so many other pressing issues to navigate. The next year, in 2012, we returned to Sarasota, but this time I took only the board secretary, Linda Kading. For the half-day session with the cabinet members, we simply Skyped them into the meeting—a marvel of technology to many of the trustees. Mission accomplished! This was the beginning of the end of the away retreat, and my time together with the board began to be more meaningful.

CHAPTER 4

THE FIRST HUNDRED DAYS: A CALL TO ACTION

Following the retreat, I hit the ground running. I was alone in an empty house, and I spent many long days in my office digging into the details of the organization. I took to heart the idea of assessing it, believing that whatever I found I would share honestly. In the back of my mind, I kept thinking that if the board did not accept my findings and perspective, "I can just go back to Meharry!" My position had not yet been filled.

It was a lonely time, made more complicated by a rental house that had major structural challenges. I had to deal with the snow that lingered into the spring and with questions from the campus about what I was doing and why. The opportunity to bring my executive assistant from Meharry to join me in Iowa helped lighten the burden—I finally had a sounding board and a confidant. Christina Henderson became my eyes and ears when I was not around. When she arrived about six weeks later, her mere presence made all the difference to me.

My first decision was to determine what to do with Steve Dengel, the former interim president. The only thing I knew about him was that he had been the CFO, then the executive vice president, and had applied for the president's job. I quickly decided to offer him the role of vice president for administrative services. He accepted.

I spent many days meeting with faculty, staff, and students in those first few months. I dug into all the documents I could find regarding operations, strategic planning, finances, etc. The board's request to assess the university's culture was a bit challenging since I was so new to the place, yet I did my best to capture its essence in my hundred-day report, which I subtitled "Actually, 88 days and counting." I wasn't sure if the board would accept my perspective, but I decided to just lay it all out there. I would be bold in my presentation and hope for the best outcome.

I began my presentation at the May 27, 2011, plenary session with the philosophy of integral leadership as defined by the Association of Governing Boards of Universities and Colleges, wherein "a president exerts a presence that is purposeful and consultative, deliberative yet decisive, and capable of course corrections as new challenges emerge— aligns the president, faculty, and the board together in a well-functioning partnership purposefully devoted to a well-defined, broadly affirmed, institutional vision." This approach resonated with me and became my foundation as I began the process of alignment. I followed this up with a situational analysis, a tool for analyzing an organization's strengths, weaknesses, opportunities, and threats.

From my eighty-eight-day perspective, I considered these to be Des Moines University's greatest strengths: a legacy of training competent and compassionate health care providers, dedicated faculty and staff, intelligent and engaged students committed to serving their community, financial stability, state-of-the-art facilities, innovative educational programming, a well-equipped simulation lab, a passionate and well-intentioned board of trustees, supportive alumni, and an institutional commitment to enhancing wellness and improving global health.

Its main weaknesses, as I saw them, were a lack of accountability and follow-through, a reluctance to seek and embrace best practices, an insufficient number of faculty members and clinical teaching sites, disparate clinical experiences in some areas, an aversion to change allied to a preference for maintaining the status quo, a failure to integrate clinics into all the academic programs, a low level of engagement with peer institutions, poor research infrastructure and training, and inadequate attention to faculty and staff development.

On the brighter side, we now had the opportunity to redefine our purpose and crystallize our identity and mission by creating a collective vision for the future. To address the challenges I found in the culture, I decided we should embrace, not avoid, difficult conversations; these would lead us to more open dialogues and the willingness to benefit from best practices and external reviews. Additional opportunities were to engage with the health care systems in town, fine-tune our research and clinical goals, and support efforts to create a diverse and inclusive educational community. We could build upon positive messages of prevention and wellness to gain national recognition, and I suggested that we start participating in debates on health care reform—in short, that we become a model of excellence in medical education.

The threats to our institution included unsustainable increases in health care spending, the uncertainty surrounding the nation's efforts to improve the health care system, and challenges to maintaining viable clinical partners and discovering fresh and sustainable revenue streams. I acknowledged the concern of competition from the opening of new schools, the pressure to attract the best and brightest students, and the possibility that faculty and staff recruitment and retention would be hampered by our inability to offer competitive salaries and other incentives. There were changing standards of accreditation, and we needed to not only meet these standards but surpass them.

Since the board had specifically challenged me to address our campus culture, I focused next on what I had observed. I quoted Jim Collins's *Good to Great: Why Some Companies Make the Leap ... and Others Don't*: "Yes, leadership is about vision. But leadership is equally about creating a climate where the truth is heard, and the brutal facts confronted." It had not taken long for me to realize a bit of hypocrisy at DMU. Overall, there appeared to be a genuine respect for others as well as a willingness to welcome everyone with friendliness and compassion. A sense of family was often used to describe the culture.

However, underneath this deceptively smooth surface, I noted pockets of passive aggression, intolerance, distrust, a fear of retribution, inequity, a reluctance to have difficult but necessary conversations, and an aversion to change. I claimed that, in order to get to a more desirable culture, we needed to concentrate on open communication, education and training, consistency, and accountability and—most important—we needed to take a vow of institutional and professional integrity.

I ended my eighty-eight-day report with a call to action focused on "where do we go from here?" I offered up a long list of next steps, beginning with a strategic planning process to be launched in a summer retreat with the board of trustees as well as the entire campus community. We needed to start by asking, Why do we exist? And where are we going? I shared the strategic planning model I had developed and used in previous institutions that identified our mission and priorities, operating principles, and long-range vision. The board acknowledged full support for moving forward together.

By the end of May, I had presented my first presidential report, had my first commencement, and experienced the horrors of major water damage and structural issues in my rental house. Although challenges were clearly on the horizon, the trustees had accepted my report, reasserted their support of my leadership, and seemed eager to follow my directive to develop a strategic plan. Only then did I feel comfortable making the decision to look for another place to live.

Divine intervention seemed to have our perfect family home—down the street and around the corner in the Glen Oaks subdivision—come on the market just as we decided to buy a house. Although we still anticipated problems selling our Nashville home, we went ahead and listed it, and within the first few weeks, we had an offer. We closed on our new home in Glen Oaks in July after selling our Nashville home. How does this happen? I accepted this as affirmation that God intended for me to be in Des Moines to lead this organization. My calling to serve.

The realization of this led my husband to announce his decision to relocate to Des Moines with his family. Luckily, Thad was able to continue working for HCA Healthcare remotely. And when he decided to branch out into his own consulting work in hospital and clinical operations, HCA became a client.

CHAPTER 5

THE BATTLE BEGINS: THE HONEYMOON ENDS

Every new president typically starts with somewhat of a honeymoon phase. You have a genuine degree of excitement—excitement that you were selected with the agreement of the entire campus community, that you were accepted by all as the right one! As a new president, you rarely know what level of competition there had been, so you start with the perception that you are the right person for the role and that the community is ready and willing to welcome your leadership.

The fact that I followed an accomplished and well-known individual who happened to be the governor of the state of Iowa *again* made for some interesting dynamics and challenges. It was awkward to follow someone of such stature who not only remained in the community, literally living down the street in the governor's mansion, but who provided leadership to the entire state. Having previously served as governor before becoming president of DMU, Terry Branstad was again in that role, and all I heard in the community upon my arrival was, "Oh, so you have big shoes to fill," and "How does it feel to follow such an accomplished leader?"

It is always daunting to be asked to appraise previous leadership, even more so when my new bosses, DMU's board of trustees, asked me for a deep assessment—as if I was doing an audit or an accreditation visit to determine the health of the organization. I took that request to heart and set out within my first few weeks on the job to do my analysis.

What I found were challenges, new and old. But if I spoke of them, I might tarnish the image of the previous leader and draw attention to a board that had failed to know about and understand the challenges of the organization.

It was a lonely start, full of trepidation, worry, and anxiety. Had I made a foolish decision to leave a comfortable role at Meharry and take on this unknown organization in the foreign land that was Des Moines? I had never imagined moving to the Midwest, and I was alone with a hope and a prayer that things would work out well.

To believe that I had been selected to do this job because of the confidence the board had in my ability to lead, then to have some members of the campus community try their best to run me away, was difficult to process. I truly believed that I was called to be a university president and that this was my purpose. And I firmly believed that without divine intervention I, Angela L. Walker Franklin, could never have imagined being selected to do this job. I was the most unlikely choice in my mind because of my own self-doubt, but I came to know that some on the board were also encouraged, yet troubled, about whether I could really be successful. And many on campus thought I would simply use this role as a stepping stone to something greater, sending the message that they didn't think their organization was worthy of an accomplished leader who would want to come and stay.

I never realized just how much kicking and screaming I would have to endure until the floodgates opened when I started making administrative changes by the fall of my first year. I had been about eight months on the job, and I knew it was time to make some changes. As the heavy lifting of assessing and evaluating all areas began, I made a point to keep a small group of board members—the executive committee—apprised of all that I found and every decision that I needed to make. That strategy would serve me well when the storms came, and the kicking and screaming turned into outright challenges to my authority.

There is a feeling that you get when you begin to realize that some people on your team are not really team players. It can be painful to reflect on this, but it comes with the territory. It was obvious in those early years that, on the surface, I had a supportive team. Behind the scenes, however, I wondered who was with me and who was against me. Your so-called street committee can help with that. You can learn a lot from casual conversations as you walk around to gain perspective on what is being said when you're not in the room. It is also helpful to have individuals whom you can rely on to bring back news in a way that informs and protects. My executive assistant, Christina Henderson, often served in that role. She was my eyes and ears when I was not around and would often give me a heads-up when I needed it.

I was also told about the silent majority—a phrase that initially bothered me because it essentially meant that some people would remain silent and not show their support of me for fear of retribution from the vocal minority. I came to learn, however, that sometimes members of the silent majority would quell an uprising just when I needed their help the most. They would not necessarily identify themselves as supporters, but nonetheless their presence made the difference.

I remember the day that my marketing and communications officer told me bluntly that she had heard that the faculty were planning to hold a vote of no confidence toward me. You can imagine the shock and worry I felt when I heard that. What concerned me most was the fact that she seemed quite casual about bringing me such news. When I asked, "Oh, my goodness, how do you know this?" she essentially said, "I have relationships with some of the faculty, and I heard that this may come up in the next faculty meeting."

What do you do with this? Frankly, I did not know what to do. The cause of the perceived attack from the faculty was likely driven by my removal of a long-standing administrator. The vocal minority chose to use this as the reason to express their disapproval about me as their president. It is still painful to recall the ugliness of this time, of being seen as an evil person who was trying to destroy the place. There was a sense that I did not know what I was doing, and they disagreed with everything I was doing. It was mostly a personnel matter, but it had undertones of a double standard. If a white male president tried the same things, would he get the same type of reaction? I wondered if the perceived attack was more about me and not so much about whether my decision was the right thing for the organization.

The vote of no confidence seemed to have been suggested often in faculty meetings by a small group. As far as I am aware, however, no vote was ever taken. The story I heard was that the silent majority helped squash the vote. So perhaps they had an impact after all.

I later learned that this battle between the people and the president had been going on for years. It was part of the culture for faculty members to be at odds with the administration. The word "transparency" was often used to mean, "You tell us everything you plan to do before you do it, and we will tell you if it is okay or not."

I spent considerable time listening to people, yet there were times when I felt under attack. The passive-aggressive behavior that I had noted in the campus culture sometimes showed itself in the open forums that I had instituted—something I called "throwing rocks, then hiding their hands." Many other times, people would directly challenge me in this open setting.

Once, shortly after this had happened in an open forum, I cited a quote about change from Jack Welch, former chairman and CEO of General Electric: "If the rate of change outside your organization is greater than the rate inside your organization, the end is in sight." In that very same presentation to the campus, I put up all the negative phrases I had been hearing, then shared a slide with all the positive, uplifting, and encouraging messages I had received from many others.

I ended with one of my favorite quotes from civil rights leader Benjamin Mays, president of Morehouse College when Martin Luther King Jr. was a student there: "It must be borne in the mind that the tragedy of life doesn't lie in not reaching your goal. The tragedy lies in having no goal to reach. It isn't a calamity to die with dreams unfulfilled, but it is a calamity not to dream. It is not a disaster to be unable to capture your ideal, but it is a disaster to have no ideal to capture. It is not a disgrace not to reach the stars, but it is a disgrace to have no stars to reach for. Not failure, but low aim."

My last slide simply stated: "I refuse to be guilty of low aim! THE SKY IS NOT FALLING!"

I wasn't sure how this message resonated with the entire campus, but a few brave souls came up to me afterward to say, "Change is hard. Many here are comfortable with who we are and where we are, and you represent change, which makes them uncomfortable." I would say this summed up my impressions quite well!

I began compiling a list of the things that had confused me when I arrived. Why did we share the minutes of my leadership team meetings with the campus? There was a faculty president at the table, but no one was there to represent the staff. What was the purpose of these meetings? How can in-house counsel deployed in general operational matters maintain objectivity when representing university interests? Where does the Des Moines University Clinic fit into the big picture? And why are people saying that I should just shut it down? My list grew longer as the days grew longer.

Perplexing things happened way too many times. Once, for example, I was approached by the strategic planning consultant who met with me in those first few months to give me the list of tasks that the strategic planning steering committee had assigned to the president. They had been waiting for me to arrive so they could hand them off to me. On the other hand, there was the offer from a long-standing administrator to allow him to continue to handle day-to-day operations, an established system that had worked well for the previous president. The things that were happening every day reminded me of the challenge of being a new leader in an environment that questioned anything and everything.

On the whole, the organization seemed satisfied with previous leaders who were just put into an administrative box that could easily be rocked or whacked on demand. I found so many times that I was being told how I should do things because it was "just the way we do things around here." And how dare I suggest raising the bar to encourage the university to reach higher goals? I was shocked to have a faculty member tell me that the university was not interested in being the best—in being at the top of any list—because "if you get too far out there, people start challenging you, and we are comfortable staying where we are." My response: "I'm sorry, but I don't think DMU's board of trustees wanted me to come here just to maintain the status quo and have the university be just a little bit mediocre."

In hindsight, I can imagine that response may not have been tactful, but I was determined to try to lead and influence an organization that was very comfortable just being what it had always been. I brought my A-game to the job, and I was ready to pull my team along, kicking and screaming. I began putting my body armor on every day when I arrived, and I reminded myself daily of the power of prayerful reflections. I asked for guidance, clear thoughts, and willing souls around me.

There were the comparisons to the previous president, for example, the perception that I wasn't seen enough on campus because the previous president would hold court in the cafeteria every day having lunch. I rarely stopped to eat in those first few months. I was driven to take it all in and set a strategy, and to stop and sit and eat was a luxury. But I realized that people wanted to know me and engage more with me, so I started setting up lunches with faculty, staff, and students. They only needed to sign up, and I would go down and have lunch with them. In the first few years, this worked well, and people came. But I guess the novelty wore off as time went on, and people stopped signing up. Perhaps they knew enough of me by then, or they just didn't care to interact with me anymore, and we stopped scheduling lunches.

When word circulated that people wanted to know if I had a dog, I considered that to be code for "We don't know enough about her." I wanted to transform DMU into an organization that operated not in an us-versus-them way but in a way that acknowledged that everyone mattered and that everyone had an opportunity to contribute to the university's overall well-being. This was a new dynamic for many people, and it was difficult to figure out how to make them see me as a caring and kind person when they also saw me removing long-standing leaders from significant roles. By the end of my second year on the job, three key administrators had been removed from their roles, and recruiting began to bring in new team members.

The prevalent view of women as leaders often came to my mind during this time. I was aware of research done by Catalyst that indicated that female leaders are typically perceived to be either friendly or competent, not both. And assertive leadership in a woman was labeled bitchy and ineffective, whereas an assertive male leader could come in and clean house one day and be lauded as a major change agent the next.

I tell the story of my early challenges at DMU not to gain sympathy or to paint a picture of me as a victim. I merely wish to share my perspective on how you can endure and how you can get to a better place when faced with adversity. Early on, of course, I doubted that I would be selected for the job, but throughout those first few years I also doubted that I could overcome the many challenges—complicated by race and gender—that I faced. But I resolved to push forward.

CHAPTER 6

FRESH IDEAS AND POSITIVE THINKING: KEY LEADERSHIP TRANSITIONS

As I continued to create my list of concerns about DMU and its structure, I sought the advice of several board members as well as the emeritus president, Dr. Richard Ryan. I also identified all the key influencers in the metropolitan area—CEOs, business leaders, philanthropists, etc.—and scheduled appointments to introduce myself. They were open and welcoming, which allowed me to get to know how the institution was perceived by community leaders. Other than hearing about its storied past as the "old D.O. school," which referred to DMU being the second-oldest college of osteopathic medicine in the country, I learned very little else.

Frankly, one key community leader indicated that he never really knew much about the university and had no idea who even served on its board. Yet they often said, "Oh, Governor Branstad was the president there, right? Did you replace him?" It became clear that this hundred-plus-year-old health sciences university had a major identity crisis with a challenging past stained by major improprieties of certain previous leaders. Once again, I vowed to correct misperceptions of who we were and emphasize the great value we had, as well as raise awareness of our institution in the community.

Defining key leadership roles formed my first set of challenges. I had often heard the phrase "a new broom sweeps clean" in relation to a new leader coming into an organization. Some new presidents would come in, clean house, and bring in their own leadership team right away. Instead, I was determined to work with the team I had inherited, then make selected changes based on needs as they evolved. My decisions were driven by team members' competency, appropriateness in their roles, and support for me as their new leader.

As I mentioned earlier, Steve Dengel, the previous executive vice president, had served for over a year as interim president and had applied for the president's job. I quickly decided to offer him the newly formed role of vice president for administrative services, overseeing IT and facilities management. I moved marketing and communications under the vice president for development and, because I could not imagine an organization that did not see human resources as paramount to its success, pulled it into administrative services. HR clearly needed a seat at the table, and I promoted its director, whose title eventually became the chief human resources officer.

The position of the dean of research, which had been housed within the College of Medicine, was already going to be reassigned to the Office of the Provost when I arrived. I clearly supported this idea, since the provost performs a university-wide function, and I supported her recommendation to name a vice president for research from within the ranks of the faculty.

Before my arrival, several audits of our information technology system had raised questions about its infrastructure and its ability to evolve with time. Seeing that years of neglect had been swept under the rug, I brought in two associates from my previous university to serve as consultants in assessing our enterprise data system and the effectiveness of our information technology system. The results were shocking and led to my immediate decision to make a leadership change in IT. I later recruited one of the consultants to the role of chief information officer.

Decisions about in-house versus general counsel were a bit more complicated. Whereas I valued the opportunity to maintain in-house counsel, the role at DMU seemed totally enmeshed in day-to-day operations, often making it difficult to determine how the university would be represented in the event of a legal challenge to decisions regarding student progress and faculty promotions or employee relations and terminations.

My list of concerns was getting longer and longer, and there were way too many issues that had legal ramifications. The opportunity to connect with the Association of Governing Boards of Universities and Colleges and its legal hotline saved me because, as a new president, I was able to get objective legal advice from a resource that was available to higher education for just this purpose.

For a new president, questioning an institution's integrity and compliance can be risky, but I needed an external, legitimate resource to evaluate and validate my findings before I acted upon them. I found this resource at the Association of Governing Boards of Universities and Colleges. This led me to decide to remove in-house counsel and engage with external counsel on matters important to a higher education institution with health sciences and clinical enterprises. We also hired the law firm SNR Denton to perform a full, privileged audit of our clinical operations, which caused me to reimagine the manner in which these operations were structured and supported within our organization.

Finding external legal counsel with no direct ties to Des Moines in order to maintain objectivity and avoid conflict of interest was my next challenge. I was advised to find external counsel outside of Des Moines and secured a seasoned higher education attorney who ably represented the university through many personnel and legal challenges. Kelly Baier of Bradley & Riley PC in Cedar Rapids and I forged a bond, and he became my close confidant in the same way that I had established good relations with several attorneys from the Association of Governing Boards of Universities and Colleges. Since our small organization, with its varied set of needs, could not be well managed by one generalist, we negotiated external counsel for labor, employment, health care, and education issues.

Attorney Kelly Baier became another reliable sounding board for me. As time went on, he helped me navigate the many delicate issues around employee relations and the need for leadership transitions. He became our go-to counsel for all things involving labor and employment law as we transitioned to other firms to advise us about health care and higher education law.

The president's cabinet that I found upon my arrival was an interesting combination of positions, to say the least. I was surprised to see that its structure included not only a small group of direct reports to the president—the provost, general counsel, chief financial officer, vice president for development, and executive vice president—but also the deans of the three colleges, the president of the faculty organization, and the vice president for student affairs. Human resources was not represented, nor was information technology services.

Before my arrival, this group met weekly with or often without the president. The cabinet appeared awkward to me; some seats at the table were filled, but other key roles were missing. The deans, reporting to the provost, were included in the cabinet but often remained silent during meetings. The power structure clearly favored a select few who seemed to call the shots.

My first decision was to make the minutes of the deliberations of the president's cabinet private. To have the minutes automatically posted to the campus community did not allow for open, honest dialogue at the meetings; key leaders needed the freedom to vet strategic priorities for the campus before sharing them. Placing marketing and communications to align with development and alumni relations was my next decision; then I created an advancement unit, changing the vice president for development to a vice president for advancement. This got a negative reaction from the marketing and communications team, a dynamic that continued to be strained for years to come.

What I learned from these early conversations about roles and functions and who worked with whom allowed me to take a step back and reimagine an environment in which we could become a highly functioning team. This led me to rename the group the Executive Leadership Team. I brought many of the units that were tucked under other units to the table—for instance, human resources, ITS, and research. Wellness was removed from reporting to student services since wellness applied to the entire campus community. I connected it to the DMU Clinic, then moved the clinic out from under finance to be a separate unit reporting directly to the president. Since I had eliminated in-house counsel, I hired a compliance officer to address our many regulatory and risk management issues.

Some would describe this period as a time of shuffling the deck or playing musical chairs, but I had a clear vision in mind, and it would take me several more steps to get there. Along the way, new individuals came into these roles as others either moved on or were transitioned out of their previous roles. Fresh ideas and positive thinking came with these shifts as we began to move forward as a team.

There were individuals who challenged my authority as I worked to define our team approach to operating as ONE university. Some units felt that they were being treated as second-class citizens, while others were perceived as receiving priority treatment.

I often heard the phrase "COM+2" used to describe the largest and oldest college, the College of Osteopathic Medicine, being treated as "golden" when the other two colleges, the College of Podiatric Medicine and Surgery and the College of Health Sciences, were considered "less than golden." It was a bothersome term that reflected a second-rate perception of these two colleges. I was determined to find a way to address this problem at some point.

As I began exploring our approach to development and fundraising, it became clear that it differed from the approach I had anticipated. We had many social functions to entertain the alumni but very little engagement with them financially. Alumni giving was less than 5 percent, and a major gift of $1,000 per year was enough to make the donor a member of the President's Society. Strategy and goal setting in advancing the organization were lacking, and the fact that past administrations had allowed giving to be tied to other amenities and promises of admission led to major integrity issues in enrollment.

Unfortunately, some engaged as donors with the hope of a favorable outcome for a friend or a relative in admission. Frankly, many of those early conversations with alumni seemed to have strings attached. Either they asked blatantly about the going rate for the year or insinuated that they would start giving now since they had a son or a daughter who would be interested in enrolling in the future.

These conversations were appalling, but they reflected a history that spanned a checkered past when deals were made under the table. I vowed to clean this up and to bring integrity into all our processes. Again, I was taking a risk by changing the culture with the hope that people would support me for doing the right thing for the benefit of the university.

CHAPTER 7

THE EXECUTIVE LEADERSHIP TEAM: CALLING OUT THE ELEPHANT IN THE ROOM

As our newly formed Executive Leadership Team evolved, I found myself with more and more direct reports. I had believed that there was a magic number of direct reports that would define best practices and efficiencies of operations. With the three deans, the vice president for enrollment management and student services, and the vice president for research all reporting to the provost and all other roles reporting to me, our duties appeared to be evenly divided. We all met weekly as one Executive Leadership Team, but there were times when the meetings seemed to splinter into another us-versus-them mentality. Those reporting to the provost were often quiet in the meetings; the deans, for example, were often reluctant to bring up items that had not yet been vetted in the provost's meeting. Nevertheless, we kept trying to build the team. Having some individuals report directly to the president and others report to the provost made for sometimes strained relationships and questionable loyalties.

Although it was a novel idea, far removed from a health sciences university, the Butler University Bulldogs basketball story became an inspiration in these early years as we learned of that team's concerted effort to pull together and defy the odds to win a national championship. The team's collaborative spirit resonated with us, and although we weren't always 100 percent in agreement, we pressed on, focusing constantly on the basic principle of treating people with respect and giving each other the benefit of the first conversation when we encountered challenges.

The old ways of burying conflicts and talking about things in the meeting only after the meeting were difficult to confront head-on. And, frankly, in those early years, I often knew that some of my direct reports were actually speaking against me in ways that seemed disingenuous. Luckily, only a few people did this. This came to light primarily when we debated new initiatives or big ideas and colleagues supported them to my face but spoke against them behind my back. The possibility of a branch medical sciences campus in Florida was just one of these ideas. Although my board members and I knew it would be a long shot, exploring possibilities when invited to consider them was only good business in my mind. It was disappointing to learn of the negative chatter regarding this idea before it was directly addressed to me in person.

Tough skin is what I would say every leader must have. Although I wasn't surprised to learn that members of my team would speak against me, I was more concerned about whom they would speak to. The most splintering thing any leadership team can do is to send a message to the organization that its leaders are not united. My challenge was to figure out how to build trust and get this team to pull together as one—to support each other for the benefit of the university.

Our organizational chart became flatter as time moved on, capturing senior leaders representing key areas of responsibility within the university.

The most puzzling thing to me, however, was the fact that people still blamed the administration for problems within the university even when some of those blamed were members of the Executive Leadership Team. To some, members of this group were not administration. "Administration" was code for the president, the CFO, and the provost. Our team was not yet pulling together as one on behalf of the university. Instead, the splintering from within the team conveyed a message of dysfunction, distrust, and a failure to coalesce around important university goals. The campus community wondered who was really calling the shots.

Our first effort in team building came with the Dale Carnegie performance management system, which I introduced to the campus in my second year on the job. It included a new approach to assessing overall institutional effectiveness by beginning with a well-defined performance plan for individuals. Beginning with the Executive Leadership Team and later encompassing all management-level staff, I used the system to prepare position results descriptions. This document identified key areas within which each performer was responsible and accountable for achieving specific results in alignment with the university's mission, vision, and strategic plan.

The three themes that evolved from the Dale Carnegie training were captured in an early conversation I had with the Executive Leadership Team: (1) Des Moines University is moving forward as a cohesive unit; (2) everyone is charged with building more linkages across the university; and (3) there is a clear focus on key results! Focusing on key results—as opposed to lists of tasks—has changed the dynamics of how we monitor progress within the organization.

Our Dale Carnegie performance training gave us a shared language centered around results and relationships. Giving individuals the opportunity to have the first conversation when there is conflict helped us begin to address issues that formerly would have been swept under the rug.

We also created an Executive Leadership Team covenant reflecting the commitment we made to each other. Its basic premises called for us to respect and value our team members, accept responsibility and constructive criticism, communicate honestly and clearly, and listen closely while collaborating and becoming visionary thinkers. See the appendix for the full document.

The Executive Leadership Team, by design, now includes the individuals responsible for key areas that affect the entire operation of the university. The deans of the three colleges, along with the leaders of important functions such as finance, enrollment, student services, academic support, human resources, research, ITS, advancement, and the clinic as well as diversity, equity, and inclusivity, are represented on the team. All members now report directly to me.

In spite of the progress we had made toward working together as a team, the usual conflicts that arise from different personalities and approaches to leadership still led to conflicts that were never brought to the surface. Over time, these festered and encouraged a culture of smiling in your face while stabbing you in the back. The psychologist in me was disappointed to know that these accomplished and well-intentioned leaders were harboring resentments that they were reluctant to discuss openly.

Even after going through the Dale Carnegie training and learning the best practice of making sure that anyone you have issues with would benefit from direct conversations, it was clear that people often sat on their hands when they should speak out. I came up with an idea that could trigger honest conversations.

The symbolism of the elephant can be used in so many different scenarios. First, how do you eat an elephant? "One bite at a time" reflects the obvious idea that you can't tackle big issues all at once, that it's best to take one small step at a time. Additionally, the idea of an elephant in the room typically refers to the fact that everyone knows about an enormous issue, but no one wants to discuss it because doing so would make someone uncomfortable.

Since I collect elephant figurines, one day I brought a lovely crystal elephant from home and placed it on the conference table in my office where we held our Executive Leadership Team meetings. It was sitting on the table when the team members arrived for our weekly meeting, and I assumed someone would mention it. No one said a word as they filed in, and the meeting began. We actually completed the meeting without any mention of this new figurine on the table where there had not been anything before.

Puzzled, I asked, "So, does anyone see anything different in the room?" They all started looking around to see if I had new pictures on the walls or new furniture on display. When I said, "No, it's on the table," one person said, "I noticed it, but I didn't think I would say anything." Another person said, "From this angle it looks like a bong given that its snout is up in the air." And then, finally, someone said, "Is that an elephant?" And, of course, I said, "YES, IT'S THE ELEPHANT IN THE ROOM!"

There was considerable laughter over the fact that they really did not even notice the elephant or want to call it out, which is exactly what we mean by the phrase. I described the symbolism of the elephant and how I wanted people to be honest about their thoughts, not sit back and harbor feelings of ill will toward anyone, and to be bold and brave enough to give constructive feedback to their colleagues when it was appropriate.

From that day forward, saying, "This is an elephant moment" or "Can I touch the elephant on this one?" or literally picking up the elephant to hold it during a difficult conversation became a way to break through the barriers to open and honest communication. The elephant is still in the room, and we have learned that the effectiveness of our team comes from our willingness to have difficult conversations and call out issues so that they don't become major challenges later on.

CHAPTER 8

ENGAGING THE CAMPUS COMMUNITY: CREATING AN INCLUSIVE CULTURE

When I arrived at Des Moines University in the spring of 2011, the institution had been around for 113 years. It began as a college of osteopathic medicine in 1898. By the early 1980s, more degrees had been added, and the name was changed to reflect its status as a university. Being called a university, however, did not necessarily mean that we functioned as a university. It was obvious to anyone looking in from the outside that the doctor of osteopathy program, historically the oldest and the largest, with the most alumni, had been and continued to be the primary focus.

However, there were two additional colleges when I arrived with two additional deans, reflecting an organization that had expanded over time with a leadership structure that resembled other universities. Additionally, the role of provost had recently been added, which provided leadership oversight to the deans of the now-three colleges: the College of Osteopathic Medicine, the College of Podiatric Medicine and Surgery, and the College of Health Sciences.

In my early conversations with the deans of these two newer colleges, they seemed to feel like stepchildren, as if they and their programs and their students did not matter as much. I understood these feelings but later began to hear them reflected in day-to-day encounters with students. The most definitive depiction of this sign of division within our own organization came when I heard of the many amenities and resources for faculty, staff, and students that were dedicated to the College of Osteopathic Medicine but were not readily available to anyone in the other colleges.

For example, I learned that the new state-of-the-art simulation center was housed in the College of Osteopathic Medicine. The center was launched with great fanfare into the community, with rich opportunities for tours and arrangements for external groups to use the space. It was brought to my attention, however, that students outside of the college sometimes had to wait to use it, or the deans had to make special arrangements to ensure that their students had equal access to this amazing teaching venue. Frankly, this was unacceptable.

The most appropriate place for this and other similar resources to reside would be in central administration, likely in the Office of the Provost, who was considered the chief academic officer. In order to make this a reality, I would have to move administrative oversight of the simulation center to the provost so that protocols could be established to allow all students and programs appropriate access to this university-wide resource. A vision for how we began operating as ONE university would be my first major hurdle. It would be a test of my ability to convince the individuals who were adamantly opposed to making any changes that this change in administrative oversight was a necessary one. Painful as it was to anticipate the battle ahead of me, I firmly believed that this was the right thing to do—that it was important to grant all students equal access to a major teaching venue.

As I began centralizing administrative oversight of academic support services, we slowly began making the transition to have Des Moines University function as one university. "ONE university" became the rallying cry that resonated throughout the campus. Of course, the deans of the College of Podiatric Medicine and Surgery and the College of Health Sciences were thrilled. The dean of the College of Osteopathic Medicine? Not so much! This set the stage for the clear ending of my honeymoon phase if I had ever really had one. The fight was staring me straight in the face, and I had a choice to make.

The decision to make a leadership change in the College of Osteopathic Medicine became the springboard to all the things that followed. In order for us to operate as one university, I had to make sure that I had leaders in all three colleges who firmly believed that we existed for all of our programs and all of our students. To grow the enterprise, we needed to grow together, respecting the needs and challenges of all of our programs and students.

Strategic visioning and planning would be my next hurdle. One of the first steps toward engaging the entire campus community called for us to define who we were. We started with WHY? Why did we exist? We began the work of creating a mission statement and setting a vision. Although university presidents are always asked to state their vision, I found it difficult, even in my inaugural address, to do much more than offer shallow, if nice, ideas about what we could be. I described big, bold, audacious goals that sounded aspirational, but at the time I had NO idea if they could ever become our reality. Instead of asserting my vision alone, it became much more important for me to work to create a collective vision—one that came from all of us.

Launching a strategic planning process was a necessary first step, and I brought to DMU a model that had worked for me in previous universities. It began with a situational analysis and the creation of a mission statement and core values, our guiding principles of engagement. It would be different from previous attempts to do strategic planning at DMU, and I remained optimistic that I could get buy-in.

In the summer of 2011, I invited Ellen Chaffee, the consultant from the Association of Governing Boards of Universities and Colleges whom I had met at that first Sarasota retreat, back to help engage the board of trustees in a strategic planning process with the university's key stakeholders. Through a very inclusive process, board members, alumni, faculty, staff, students, and I created a mission statement, established core values, and set the stage for creating a university vision statement and goals that focused on four key areas: educational excellence, clinical service, research, and community outreach and public health.

Later that year, we all coalesced around the mission statement that lives with us today: "We exist to improve lives in our global community by educating diverse groups of highly competent and compassionate health professionals." We continue to affirm that succinct statement every three years as we assess and evaluate our progress. Through this process, we also established the core values that serve as our guiding principles: accountability, collaboration, honesty, inclusiveness, and wellness.

This began the process of changing Des Moines University's culture as we engaged the entire campus community. Our core values of accountability, collaboration, honesty, inclusiveness, and wellness continue to resonate with everyone today. As we evolved into a unified community, "everyone matters," "everyone is welcome," and "everyone is seen and respected" became our rallying cries.

I came to DMU well equipped to launch strategic plans and establish goals for the future. What you often hear, however, is the phrase "culture eats strategy for lunch," which essentially means that if you do not focus on understanding and building a more collaborative and respectful culture where people feel they matter, you can forget about trying to establish an effective plan for the future. I also found this phrase informative: "People don't care what you know until they know that you care." I kept this phrase very much in mind in my early years at DMU when I realized that I needed to find a way not only to establish university-wide core values but to really embrace them as guiding principles that would permeate the campus community.

There was more work to do when I arrived than I imagined there would be. My mere presence as the first woman and the first person of color to lead the university spoke to the issues of racial diversity and inclusivity. My presence triggered reactions from many because I was unlike anyone else who had ever led the institution.

Some were inspired to acknowledge that DMU had not done a great job in diversifying its student body. When I asked them about this, I learned that there had been little discussion about creating a diversity plan, although accreditation bodies often asked about these efforts. Besides the fact that DMU did not have a diversity plan, some were concerned the university had not made a deliberate attempt to diversify the health professions workforce. There had been an attempt to establish a scholarship fund for minority students from underrepresented backgrounds, called the Glanton Scholarship fund, but few students had been recruited and awarded the scholarship.

Having been at other health sciences universities, I was aware of the targeted efforts that other universities made to attract talented students. However, at DMU, there was an assumption that we could not get those students to consider coming to Iowa. When I arrived, I began challenging that assumption. After all, I chose to come to Iowa and to DMU because of the manner in which I was recruited by the individuals who hired me. I was not surprised to hear, however, once we started talking about creating a diversity plan, that we were doing so only because we had an African American president. Clearly, there was much more work to be done than I had imagined.

I decided to focus on setting a framework to begin talking about the value we place on the environment we create for others. Because the board of trustees had made such a concerted effort to welcome me, and because people tend to go where they feel supported, I pressed DMU to work to provide this same hospitable environment in order to attract and retain individuals from diverse backgrounds.

This simple idea reminded me of a phrase from the medical field that can be traced back to the nineteenth-century French chemist Louis Pasteur. Simply stated, "It is not the seed, it is the soil."

I believe we must focus more on our environment to cultivate and embrace the value added by diverse perspectives as opposed to just recruiting individuals from diverse backgrounds to add to our ranks.

Until a culture is open and welcoming, adding individuals from diverse backgrounds will not change its dynamic. If someone does not feel welcome, that individual will likely not thrive. Recruitment may be successful, but retention will be compromised.

I pressed DMU to provide this vital environment. Changing the culture and the environment must begin with us looking within to assess our own biases and stereotypical thinking so that we can have open, honest dialogues about how different perspectives make us all enriched, valued, and respected.

This approach flourished after I created the role of director of multicultural affairs in 2012 and recruited Dr. Rich Salas, an accomplished academician who was well equipped to bring expertise in programming intended to diversify the health professions workforce. By embracing a broad definition of diversity in all its dimensions of race, ethnicity, gender, sexual orientation, socioeconomic status, age, physical ability, and religious and political beliefs, we are well on our way to establishing a national reputation for excellence in diversity, equity, and inclusivity in health professions training.

Starting with DMU's first strategic plan, Vision 2015, we have engaged in a collaborative process every three years to affirm our mission and core values and review and update our goals and strategies for the next three years. These center around areas of key results: educational excellence, clinical training, research, community outreach and advocacy, and diversity, equity, and inclusivity. We then use our overarching goals as the backdrop for college and unit operational plans and strategies.

This approach now functions as a well-oiled machine as we continue to affirm and reflect on our strategies in an active and engaged process. Accreditation expectations are now easily met, and we have a campus culture that reflects DMU's determination to value mission-based and collaborative work to achieve its goals. Everyone can take pride in knowing that the work they do contributes to the progress that the university is making in its overall institutional effectiveness.

The big, bold, audacious goals I offered in my inaugural address in 2011 may have sounded aspirational at the time but were really close to being pie in the sky. Today, however, we have achieved them in a manner that no one could have imagined, perhaps because we started by believing that it was possible for us to achieve them.

Our core values and inclusive culture served us well when the world shut down in March 2020. We quickly mobilized the campus to shelter in place, converting all teaching to online instruction and reimagining clinical training in a virtual platform. Most clinical students were removed from hospital and clinical settings, and we knew that in order to have them readmitted to continue their clinical training, it was our responsibility to have them properly protected. Investing in PPE became a necessary budget item, and we made sure that everyone was well equipped to be in the presence of others.

When we began returning to campus, our protocols included masks, spacing, small groups, and full PPE—masks, gowns, and shields for everyone. Our clinical services continued to provide care, and we never closed the campus, keeping it open for students who needed access to a stable network and dedicated space to continue their online instruction. When vaccines became available, we mobilized a team to make sure that our clinic could become a site for the community.

What made the difference was the fact that we have always worked collaboratively. Shifting to a virtual Zoom platform allowed us to meet as usual and continue to debate and determine the best way forward for our campus community. I firmly believe that our successful navigation of the pandemic was due to the fact that we had already learned how to play well in the sandbox together. The fears and concerns about dealing with the unknown were real, but we stayed focused on the most important things: our people and our mission. We stayed the course.

President Franklin's inauguration drew a 50-passenger bus of family and friends from McCormick, South Carolina, her hometown, as well as Atlanta, Georgia, and Nashville, Tennessee. Her parents, Hervey Wesley Walker Jr. and Leola Grant Walker, provided the bus, which arrived at DMU in time for a campus picnic on Sept. 23, 2011.

President Franklin's parents, Hervey Wesley Walker Jr. and Leola Grant Walker, taught their daughter to value and pursue education and to live by the Golden Rule.

Building relationships with DMU's governing board was and is President Franklin's early and ongoing priority. In this photo she is in the front row, center, at her first President's Society gala as DMU's president in December 2011. The event was held at Terrace Hill, the historic Iowa governor's mansion, thanks to then-Gov. Terry Branstad, who served as DMU's 14th president. Shown with President Franklin are DMU Board members (front row) Richard Kotz, D.O.; James Grekin, D.O., MACOI; Larry Baker, D.O., FACEP; Art Wittmack, M.B.A.; (second row) Steve Morain, J.D.; Arthur Angove, D.O. (gray tie); Max McKinney II, D.O.; (third row) Gilbert Bucholz, D.O., FAOCR; Mary Radia, D.O.; Jacqueline Stoken, D.O., FAAPMR, FAOCPMR; (back row) Chip Finch, D.O., FACOEP; Bernard Feldman, D.O., FACG; Victoria Herring, J.D.; and Susan Beck, D.O., FACOS.

Richard Ryan Jr., D.Sc., the 13th president of DMU, was among the honored guests at President Franklin's inauguration as DMU's 15th president and CEO on Sept. 24, 2011.

Shown here with then-DMU Board of Trustees chair James Grekin, D.O., MACOI, left, and fellow board member Larry Baker, D.O., FACEP, President Franklin donned the DMU medallion before her inauguration as DMU's 15th president and CEO on Sept. 24, 2011.

President Franklin and her friend and mentor, Louis W. Sullivan, M.D., at the university's Commencement in 2016. Sullivan gave the keynote address at the event.

Among President Franklin's achievements at DMU has been raising awareness about the university's Glanton Fund, which supports diversity, equity and inclusion programming and scholarships for students with diverse backgrounds. The fund is named after the late Judge Luther Glanton and Willie Stevenson Glanton, two Central Iowa attorneys, civil rights leaders and DMU Board of Trustees members. Here, President Franklin talks with Willie Glanton at the university's annual Glanton Event in 2012.

President Franklin has worked to increase support for DMU's Glanton Fund, which supports scholarships and diversity, equity and inclusion programming at the university. Here, she and husband Thaddeus Franklin Jr., M.H.A., attend the 2018 Glanton Event, an annual fundraiser for the fund, with DMU students Mohamad Hassan, Sondos Masoud and Ruffin Tchakounte.

President Franklin and her husband, Thaddeus Franklin Jr., M.H.A., celebrate the public kickoff of DMU's Purple & Proud Campaign on Dec. 8, 2018. The campaign began with a $25 million goal, but after that was surpassed, DMU doubled the goal to $50 million in 2020. That goal was exceeded in January 2024.

The Franklin family, from left: Jordan, Angela, Thaddeus, Grant, daughter-in-law Karen Franklin and Wesley. Karen and Wesley's daughter, Harper, stands in front.

The Franklin family, from left: husband Thaddeus Franklin Jr., M.H.A., President Franklin; son Grant; her parents, Hervey Wesley Walker Jr. and Leola Grant Walker; son Jordan; daughter-in-law Karen and her husband, son Wesley.

In 2019, Mark Peiffer, M.B.A., CPA, DMU senior vice president and chief financial officer, and President Franklin met at the McKinney Law Offices at the suggestion of the late attorney Bill Lillis, J.D., to discuss purchasing 88 acres in West Des Moines from the McKinney family for DMU's new campus. Lillis served as legal counsel for the university and facilitated the DMU leaders' initial contact with the family.

DMU Board Chair Michael Witte, D.O., and University President Angela Walker Franklin — seated, fourth and third from right, respectively — sign the purchase agreement for 88 acres of the McKinney family's property for the new campus on May 24, 2019. They were joined by DMU trustees and members of the McKinney family to celebrate the historic moment.

President Franklin shares information about DMU's plan to move its campus to West Des Moines during a news conference in June 2019.

President Franklin and other DMU leaders visit the new campus site on Sept. 18, 2019, when the last building on the property was demolished.

President Franklin was joined by DMU Board of Trustees members Mary Radia, D.O.; Dave Kapaska, D.O., M.B.A.; Renee Hardman, M.B.A., SPHR; Larry Baker, D.O., FACEP; and Michael Witte, D.O., for the Sept. 10, 2020, groundbreaking of the university's new campus.

President Franklin and her husband, Thaddeus Franklin Jr., M.H.A., visit the new campus.

At a special Sept. 10, 2021, event, President Franklin and her husband, Thaddeus Franklin Jr., M.H.A., added their signatures to a 2,304-pound beam that made its permanent home in the uppermost southwest corner of the Innovation building on the new West Des Moines campus. Before it was put in place, the beam was transported to DMU's 3200 Grand Ave. campus so that students and employees could also sign it.

New campus steering committee members Vickie Harper, business operations analyst; Stephanie Greiner, M.S., vice president of university advancement; John Harris, director of facilities management; and Mark Peiffer, M.B.A., CPA, senior vice president and chief financial officer, observe construction with President Franklin in September 2021.

New campus steering committee members Mark Peiffer, M.B.A., CPA, senior vice president and chief financial officer; Stephanie Greiner, M.S., vice president of university advancement; and John Harris, director of facilities management, accompanied President Franklin on Nov. 15, 2021, when the Innovation building was "topped off" with the autographed beam.

Despite the worldwide COVID-19 pandemic, construction continued on the new campus, pictured here in December 2021.

President Franklin and the new campus steering committee members visit the new campus in February 2022. From left: President Franklin; Mark Peiffer, M.B.A., CPA, senior vice president and chief financial officer; Vickie Harper, business operations analyst; John Harris, director of facilities management; and Stephanie Greiner, M.S., vice president of university advancement.

The DMU Board of Trustees presented President Franklin with a special sign for the new campus at a Sept. 16, 2022, event of the DMU President's Society, which honors donors of $1,000 or more to the university annually. "Franklin Way" now marks the road through the West Des Moines campus. "McKinney Farm Road" honors the family from whom the university purchased land for the campus and marks the road on its western edge.

In December 2022, members of the DMU Board of Trustees, Executive Leadership Team and the new campus steering committee joined President Franklin for a tour of the new campus.

President Franklin joined the processional at DMU's 123rd Commencement in 2023.

President Franklin chats with DMU students.

President Franklin meets with DMU students in the Innovation building on the West Des Moines campus.

CHAPTER 9

LESSONS IN LEADERSHIP: HOW DO YOU BUILD TRUST WITH STRANGERS?

There is a clear understanding that strong relationships are built on a foundation of trust. Mutual respect and compassion are the other legs of this three-legged stool. Respect and compassion can be brought to the table on day one, yet trust takes time. Ronald Reagan often used the Russian proverb "trust but verify" (ironically, he used it when discussing U.S. relations with the Soviet Union), which essentially makes us aware that before we consider a source of information to be trustworthy, information from that source should be verified and deemed unquestionably true and accurate. For me, the saying signals that even if all appears to be in order, the jury's still out. It will take time before we can come to a final verdict and validate the assumptions we have made.

There are so many books on effective leadership that it is often difficult to discern whether any particular theory or approach really makes any difference. How you define success in leadership is equally elusive—what may be perceived to be effective and successful in one setting may be perceived to be fairly common in another.

Every leader of an organization goes into the role hoping to make an impact. A positive impact! We all aspire to do our jobs well and to be recognized for making a difference in the lives of those we serve. For me, this idea of service is what defines my approach to leadership. In all my many roles, I have seen my primary role as being of service. As a trained psychologist, I served my patients, hoping to guide them through their life transitions. As a faculty member, I served my students, imparting knowledge for their future edification. As an academic administrator, I served my university, having an effect on overall operational efficiencies and protocols. Pursuing a college presidency grew out of my genuine desire to continue to be of service at the highest levels of an organization. What I brought to this leadership role was the same level of commitment and humility that defined all my other roles. I did not become a president to stand out but to continue to serve.

Some come to leadership with natural instincts, whereas others need to develop them along the way. I often share a message of "first know thyself" with any aspirational leader. Who we are and how we come to our roles make all the difference. The fundamental premise is respect and compassion for others. If nothing else, the relationships we develop with others make all the difference in how we are perceived as leaders. Demonstrating a consistent message of respect and compassion—and thereby treating people with kindness—is the foundation of any successful relationship. Being the leader just means that you have that many more people to convince.

"Leadership" is a word that is often described, analyzed, and debated. Everyone seems to have a theory about what makes a good leader. And leaders are typically judged by others based on whether they ascribe to a particular approach. Right or wrong, we tend to make judgment calls about the effectiveness of leaders based on whether we think they are following the "right" approach.

I, too, have described, analyzed, and debated the definition of effective leadership, using my own life experiences to shape what I believe works for me. When asked about my philosophy of leadership, I usually start by sharing the principles of servant leadership drawn from Robert Greenleaf's 1970 essay "The Servant as Leader." Servant leadership is basically an approach that focuses on active engagement, collaboration, and respect for others. "To serve … not to be served."

There is such variation in work environments that it is impossible to recommend a one-size-fits-all approach to effective leadership. What works in one environment may not work in other environments, which is why I think it is more important to talk about personal style and attributes as opposed to theory and philosophy. So, instead of focusing on a particular theory, I tend to consider basic attributes that I think go hand in hand with great leadership skills.

At the top of my list of essential ingredients for effective leadership is authenticity. Being authentic is one of the guiding principles that I choose to follow, and I also expect this in others. Honesty, genuineness, and trustworthiness also belong with this principle. I see modeling genuine authenticity as a true test of leadership. It is an essential ingredient for successful leadership, yet getting everyone to agree and demonstrate it may be an ongoing challenge. I see it as an aspirational workplace goal. To aim for anything less is a breeding ground for distrust and deceit.

If you are doing it right, being authentic requires a certain amount of vulnerability, transparency, and integrity. Our thoughts and feelings become visible. In most relationships, personal and work, we have thoughts and feelings that we may or may not want to disclose. Of course, no one should be expected to reveal all, yet there is value in getting to a place where people feel comfortable in their own genuineness. Without it, we will continue to ignore the elephants in the room.

While it can be quite difficult to be authentic in our personal relationships with friends and family, it can be even more challenging in our work environment. In some work cultures, there is a tendency to sugarcoat problems, even though ignoring them could be destructive. Failure to have difficult conversations is usually the cause. A test of leadership is an ability to get everyone comfortable enough with each other so that having these difficult conversations is not seen as belittling or disrespectful.

If you remember first to treat others the way that you would want to be treated, then it is important to start from a place of genuine concern and respect for them. Leaders should strive to create a safe zone of interaction—a safe zone where we can have difficult conversations, acknowledge obvious conflict, and do this in a way that allows feelings to be put aside for the good of the organization. This may be a day-to-day challenge, but it is an institutional imperative. It gets better with time as trust builds.

As a new leader, you are likely the newest member of the organization, and you enter highly esteemed. All who look up to you as their new leader have their own expectations, concerns, and worries about the paths you may take. You are also entering a well-established culture that is understood by those who live in it. You have a sense of stumbling in the dark, of making assumptions about the culture and its people, often with very sketchy and inaccurate details.

With the arrival of any new leader comes the honeymoon phase, when the excitement of something new carries the day. If the new leader brings positive energy with a sincere attempt to build rapport, this phase typically goes well. It unravels slowly in most cases, but it typically comes to an abrupt end when the new leader makes the first change in the status quo.

Whereas most would assume that a new leader is likely to change something, there is an expectation that change would be slow and would definitely not affect MY area of responsibility. I find it important, however, for a new leader not to wait too long to make the first change. The thick skin that must come with the role has to be intact because that first move may be the kiss of death. Acquiring an understanding of the culture and the dynamics of the relationships—who is connected to whom—is important.

At DMU, I took the time to understand the relationships, but regardless, once I caused the first transition of a key leader, the campus sat on the edge of their metaphorical seats, wondering and waiting. "WHAT will she do next?" "WHO does she think she is?" "She doesn't know what she's doing." "She will destroy the place."

That first disruption! It didn't take long for the honeymoon phase to come to an end when I made that first move. Suddenly, I went from being the person who was welcomed with open arms and smiles to being the person who was given the side-eye and the rolled eye. And there was way too much blank eye, blank stares that made it difficult for me to tell whether anyone would continue to support me.

It was perhaps a slow transition, but to me it felt abrupt. The one saving grace was the bond I had formed with the board of trustees, perhaps because I started with a genuine desire to be open and honest with them about my every move. When major decisions had to be made, I painted a clear picture, explained my rationale, and then offered details about the execution of my plan. This was sometimes painful for them, yet as time went on, they began to trust my instincts and my willingness to make tough calls and act on them.

Character and integrity go hand in hand as we define the basic traits of effective leaders. Typically, people are considered to have good characters if they show signs of integrity, honesty, fortitude, loyalty, and the other important virtues that promote good behavior. These character traits define who they are as people and influence the choices they make in their lives. I would add compassion and empathy as well to this list of essential ingredients. There is nothing uniquely special about these traits in the leadership realm. I am essentially saying that to be a great leader you simply need to be perceived to be a good person, one who cares for others, who is honest and trustworthy, and who is eager to live a life where people are treated humanely and respectfully.

It should go without saying, but the first step toward being an effective leader is to be a good person. The best way that I believe we can describe this is to think first of the Golden Rule—treating everyone the way we would want to be treated.

Our life experiences are uniquely us. Whereas some may follow similar career paths and may have comparable life experiences, the manner in which we process those experiences may be vastly different from one person to the other. There may be a traditional pathway to leadership roles, but depending on the industry, one person may toil in the trenches for years before an opportunity for advancement appears. In contrast, others may leapfrog over some of the steps if an opportunity presents itself and they are well positioned to step up and lead.

So, there is no one-size-fits-all approach to effective leadership. However, how we learn from our experiences and how we build upon them to form an approach and a strategy for our next career journey can make all the difference. Resiliency can best be described as the capacity to recover quickly from difficulties. The longer you live, the more likely it is that obstacles will be placed in your path. How well you deal with these obstacles will define how easy or how difficult your path will be.

I often describe my approach to navigating through challenges as putting up my shield and putting on my body armor. Envisioning an extra layer of protection so things did not penetrate my defenses was my approach. I would actually visualize strapping on this extra layer (as Superman may do going into the phone booth), then coming out ready for action. It was a deliberate attempt to prepare my mind and my body for the potential attack, to be ready for it just in case. It was a mental exercise, more than anything else, to remain cool, calm, and collected even in the most challenging of times.

This trait may be innate to me, but the strategy can be easily taught—there are many descriptions of ways to stop, take a deep breath, and calm yourself in stressful times. "Relax, relate, release" is a phrase often used in similar circumstances. It may not come instinctively, but being mindful of this strategy can make a difference both in the way that you show up for a challenge and in the perception that people then have of how well you handled the situation.

There were times in my first few years at DMU when I faced swirling accusations of not being transparent enough to explain why I had made certain decisions. When personnel decisions are made, those clearly must remain confidential, but I was often called upon in a most inappropriate and unprofessional manner to explain myself. I recall being summoned by a group of faculty and students to appear in a classroom to explain why I had made a major change in administrative leadership.

At first, I wondered if this kind of challenge was typical in this environment, because I could not ever have imagined demanding explanations of a president. I accepted the invitation to appear before this group and went down to answer their questions. When it became clear that most of their questions could not be answered, I explained carefully what I could and could not share with them, thanked them for their time, then walked out.

Some who saw me navigate that encounter wondered how in the world I maintained my composure—how did I avoid getting into a shouting match or accusing them all of being out of line and disrespectful? Frankly, my impression was that those who were bold enough to make such a demand would have been pleased to see me explode, which would fuel the fire of their impressions of me as harsh, inappropriate, and difficult to work with—evidence they could use to prove that I was not right for the role. I didn't give them what they wanted but confused them by being direct, matter of fact, and unflappable. I use the phrase "never let them see you sweat" to describe how I navigated that challenge. Inside, however, my blood was boiling.

CHAPTER 10

THE VITAL DYNAMIC: CONFRONTATION, VALIDATION, AND THE BOARD OF TRUSTEES

I have mentioned my relationship with the board of trustees as being vital to my success. They were the individuals who took a chance by saying both "Yes, you are the one" and "We believe we can trust you to tell us what we don't already know."

Thanks to my many career development workshops, including the ACE Fellows Program, I was aware of the real importance of establishing good relationships with my new bosses, this board of trustees. I had been privy to relationships between presidents and boards in my two previous organizations, and I clearly knew the power of this dynamic—how it could go really well and how it could turn horribly wrong.

I often remarked that I learned mostly how NOT to be a president from my previous encounters. I hoped to start out on the right foot with my new bosses and gain their respect and trust. And, frankly, at the time I still doubted whether I had made the right decision to come to Des Moines. I was a bit fearful of the challenge, yet I pressed on because at some level I really believed it was divine intervention—otherwise, no one would ever have expected me to be here to do the things I was asked to do. The fact that I was offered the job of being the fifteenth president of this 113-year-old health sciences university in the heart of the Midwest, so far away from family and friends, must have been ordained.

At least that's what I told myself. Being prayerful and holding on to my faith, especially after reading Rick Warren's book *The Purpose Driven Life*, I reminded myself often that this was a calling, that my true purpose was to be realized in this role of being president of DMU. I held on to that belief and that faith as I began my journey here.

I relied heavily on materials from the Association of Governing Boards of Universities and Colleges and quoted its philosophy of integral leadership in my first meeting with the board after I became president. I wanted to set the stage and create an aspirational future state that was steeped in best practices. In the association's words: "Whether an institution is public or private, large or small, four-year or two-year, the compelling need is for the chief executive who can demonstrate integral leadership."

This definition of integral leadership became the basis for how I would proceed. More than anything, I clearly understood that my first task was to answer the call of the board and build a trusting relationship with them. The board members were the ones who had hired me to do the job of leading the organization. They clearly had confidence in me, yet I needed to make sure that we all thought that their decision was the right decision. I knew they would assess my performance. At the same time, I was wondering whether I had made the right choice and whether they would support me in the role.

The value I placed on my relationship with the board proved to be essential to my longevity and success in the role. Trust was the foundation of our relationship, and this trust came from a place of mutual respect. My tactics were simple: keep the board in the loop on all matters pertinent to the operation of the organization, apprise them of problems and never allow them to be blindsided, seek their affirmation and constructive feedback on key decisions, be open and honest in sharing perspectives but be a great listener as well, ask for advice and be respectful, and share your visionary dreams to get their buy-in.

I often tell aspiring leaders that I learned the most about becoming a university president by seeing how others failed in the role. It had become clear to me that the path to success in such a role began and ended with the dynamics built with the board of trustees. This did not mean that I saw building relationships with staff, faculty, and students as secondary. It just meant that I knew the first order of business was to make sure that I was transparent and informative in my engagements with the board. They needed to know that they could trust me and that I would always be open and honest with them—even when the news I needed to share was difficult.

When the board asked me to do a hundred-day assessment and report my findings at the May 2011 meeting, this allowed me to dig deeply and share my perspective honestly, knowing that this gave me permission to tell them what I truly found and believed to be true about the university. There was comfort in knowing that they wanted to know what I thought, and I could always say, "Well, you asked for the truth."

I also took comfort from the fact that I could and should be bold in my report. If they accepted my boldness and didn't ask me to leave, that would be the way I would continue to engage with them. And that is exactly what happened. They responded positively, and I ended the board meeting with a renewed sense of excitement for the role and a commitment from the board to support me in transforming the organization.

I learned things from this early assessment that would warrant changes that I knew would be controversial. As I began making these changes, particularly in leadership, some board members grew weary of the growing noise on campus and began targeting the provost as the source of most of this noise. The backlash to me as the new president came from some faculty members who believed that my decision to keep the provost while removing the dean of the College of Osteopathic Medicine was inappropriate. Some saw her as the problem, not the dean. Given that the dean was tightly connected with many board members, this became a delicate dance. One member who served as CEO of a major hospital system dramatically resigned from the board, apparently in protest of my decision to remove this dean. The fallout continued with a few other alumni serving on the board.

My worst and most challenging year as president was 2012–13 as I dealt with the aftermath of this decision and many of the other leadership transitions. Although the support that I received from my board was golden and reassuring, the day-to-day challenges were unrelenting. And as if this wasn't stressful enough, the year of the turmoil on campus was also the scheduled year for ModernThink's Great Colleges to Work For survey, the campus-wide employee satisfaction survey. I was adamantly opposed to delaying the survey and decided to just grit my teeth and wait for the final shoe to drop. I presumed I would be slaughtered in the survey.

In partnership with the *Chronicle of Higher Education*, ModernThink founded the Great Colleges to Work For program in 2008. Its mission is to help colleges and universities become better places to work and learn; its survey gathers feedback from employees designed to give leaders the information they need to drive strategic change. Rich Boyer, founding partner of ModernThink, was assigned to DMU, and meeting him was a breath of fresh air. Having engaged with many colleges and universities around the country, he shared the results of the 2013 survey with a balanced perspective. It was too easy for me to go straight to the written remarks where individuals can freely attack anyone and everyone. If you were to read the things that were said about me, you would think they were talking about the devil in disguise. It was hurtful, and some of those individuals may still be employed at DMU today.

However, Rich Boyer helped me look at the big picture. Frankly, the survey results captured more positive energy and positive statements than I had initially thought. He also put it in perspective, acknowledging that he had seen worse in other organizations and that the amount of venom spewed at me as president, given the bold leadership changes, was not unexpected. To my surprise, however, the survey included comments that showed support for these long-overdue decisions. I felt a sense of calm for the first time in months, no longer worrying that I had to keep looking over my shoulder to make sure I would not be attacked.

Using students as weapons against the president was probably the most shocking problem I encountered in those early years. Faculty members fed negativity about me and my decisions to students, which caused them to speak against me. A small minority of faculty threatened to hold a vote of no confidence in my leadership. Many faculty and students sent negative statements and bogus survey results reflecting the minority opinion of my effectiveness to board members, which caused two members to disrupt board meetings with a call to act against me.

Through it all, I gained a considerable degree of respect for the core group of board members who were determined to do the right thing and not allow this minority opinion to disrupt their deliberations. I recall the day during a board meeting in 2013 that Dr. Jim Grekin, chairman of the board, asked me to step out of a plenary session. I came back to my office and told Christina Henderson, my executive assistant, "Well, I guess this is it this time. They are talking about some issue a board member wanted to bring up." A few minutes later, I was summoned back into the boardroom.

Dr. Grekin announced that he was not going to stand for board members who raised unfounded claims about my leadership based on fraudulent surveys that clearly came from a few individuals who were against me. He announced, "From the very beginning, we selected our president because we truly believe she is the person who will help this institution transform into something we have always wanted: a highly accomplished and recognized institution of higher learning. Those of us who get constant updates from the president not only understand why decisions needed to be made, but we also believe they were long overdue. So, if there is any board member here today who cannot support this president, they can leave now." One board member got up, walked out, and never returned. I was aware of another member who remained seated but who was later asked to leave the board or be removed.

Of all the support I received from the board, this was the biggest "WOW" moment for me. I sometimes look back on that time and wonder how I made it to the other side. The board never wavered in their support of me, which is truly remarkable. They trusted my judgment, and I kept them informed constantly about the challenges I faced and the manner in which I needed to navigate change. Coming out of this, I knew there would remain a small minority of individuals who wanted me out of the role, but I was encouraged to know that many more were hopeful and supportive.

I vowed to spend my time focusing on building upon that level of support to allow people to get to know me as me, not as the person whom others tried to paint as destined to destroy the place. I found all the negativity toward me insulting, but I knew it came from a place of fear of the unknown and fear of change. It would take several more leadership changes, as well as new leadership in the College of Osteopathic Medicine, to finally calm the waters.

The first new dean of that college in 2013 affirmed the position I had taken and allowed the faculty to come to the realization of the need for change. Building rapport with this new dean, based on mutual respect, was the turning point for me. Unfortunately, his early departure just two years later to pursue an amazing national role opened the door for additional scrutiny about the stability of the organization and the overall effectiveness of my presidency once again. A few interims and a second failed hire a few years later made it difficult to calm the naysayers.

A local medical association added fuel to the fire by choosing to circulate again a negative view of my effectiveness as a leader, which caused fresh doubts to spread throughout the osteopathic community. The ultimate confrontation came when one of our own alumni raised concerns with the secretary of the national accrediting body, the Commission on Osteopathic College Accreditation, to question the turnover in the dean's office at DMU.

With the help of DMU's legal counsel and the full support of the DMU board of trustees, we sent a proper admonishment to the commission for crossing a line into staffing and personnel as opposed to accreditation standards. Our pushback essentially questioned the commission's authority to assess our leadership roles and decisions. And in spite of the turnover in the dean's office, our student outcomes had exceeded all projections, thanks primarily to the dedicated engagement of the faculty. They were the true custodians of the high-quality educational programs that we offered.

This was a real sore spot for me because I was aware of the degree of turnover in administrative roles in other osteopathic colleges that had not received the same level of scrutiny. This was yet another example of microaggression intended to paint me as an ineffective leader compared with other presidents, with the same amount of turnover, who were considered to be change agents.

My original presidential contract called for the standard three years. Early on, I created a presidential assessment protocol that I adopted from the Association of Governing Boards of Universities and Colleges. Although previous presidents had received a less formal review process, I knew there was a greater chance that I would be treated differently. I had heard too many horror stories of presidents getting into the crosshairs with board members, and I was determined to set some parameters upon which I would be judged and evaluated.

As I approached my third year, I asked for a comprehensive presidential assessment from the Association of Governing Boards of Universities and Colleges. My then-chair, Dr. Larry Baker, and I attended the association's annual meeting in spring 2014 as we launched the process. This internal-external 360-degree review was exactly what I needed. A sense of vulnerability came with it, but I was determined to learn from it and move on. I needed the external validation, and I got it thanks to the association's consultant, Dr. Carol Cartwright, who reported to the board at its May meeting that I was effective in my role.

That was the affirmation I needed, and I was then awarded a new contract for six years ending in May 2020. My thoughts were that a nine-year successful presidency at DMU would position me well for the next opportunity somewhere out there. I had weathered the storm, survived a major threat to my authority, and gained some personal wins along the way.

CHAPTER 11

AN ENTIRELY NEW CAMPUS: MOBILIZING OUR COMMUNITY

At the start of my second contract, I finally felt vindicated and validated as an effective leader. It was now time for DMU to move into a phase of growth and opportunity. Fundraising was our next big hurdle, and we sought external consultation to do a feasibility study of prospects for a major campaign. The results were not good. Not only was it determined that I did not have a strong enough level of giving among board members, but the alumni base also resisted engaging or giving beyond their current level.

My chief advancement officer, Stephanie Greiner, and I decided that it was still worth a try and that we would defy the odds. We launched the Purple and Proud campaign anyway. This was the first major campaign of this type in the university's history, and we went public in December

2018, already having received $17 million toward our $25 million goal. In 2018, I had also hired a new provost, anticipating that if I were to leave at the end of my contract period, there would be talent within the organization to consider as part of a presidential succession plan. In fact, I had presumed that my departure would coincide with the successful culmination of Purple and Proud. As fate would have it, however, shortly after we went public with our campaign, everything changed.

We ended the calendar year 2018 with grand fanfare that was quickly sidetracked by a simple request to rezone one acre of land we owned behind the campus to allow for a generator and an extension of parking. Over the years, with sporadic power outages in Ryan Hall, the building housing the animal care facility and research labs, we were concerned about compromising research studies in our developing research enterprise. This was the one building on campus that needed a generator, and we needed to place it on land behind that building. We also hoped to expand our parking lot to get approximately fifty more spaces to address the parking challenges on campus, given that more of our students were now living over a mile away and weren't able to walk to campus.

As we contemplated a need for a zoning change, we worked diligently to address a decades-long problem due to the university's failure to maintain a detention pond in the back lot—the neighbors behind us worried about water runoff and flooded basements whenever there was any construction on campus. We saw this as a legitimate responsibility for DMU, and we invested nearly $1 million in upgrading the detention basin with protocols for maintenance approved by the City of Des Moines. Additionally, we chose to engage with the neighborhood association to make sure they were aware of the upgrades and our concerns for their properties.

The surprise came in the first planning and zoning meeting in December 2018. The meeting had to be aborted when one member had to leave, and they lost quorum. The noise from the audience, however, gave us pause. Was there a movement within the neighborhood to resist our request? Little did we know that this would be the beginning of the firestorm that led us to decide to relocate the campus.

We mobilized our campus community to present our best case for the need for the rezoning by asking students and faculty to join us at the rescheduled January 2019 meeting. Legal representation from attorney Bill Lillis, as well as a carefully crafted opening statement, was part of the plan. The outcome of this meeting still brings chills as I recall the level of incivility and unprofessionalism that came from many of the neighbors who showed up. The noise from the neighborhood and the concerted opposition to our plan led to the complete rejection of our request to rezone the one-acre plot.

That decision had several effects on me. For one, I vowed to NEVER take my campus community into such a bloodbath again. The yelling and cheering in the room from adults determined to derail our plan were shocking. The disparaging comments made toward me as president were appalling. The neighborhood association presented a document signed by a former DMU administrator promising to never expand beyond the current footprint. That was the death knell that caused the planning and zoning members to berate me and DMU for not being good neighbors.

I was embarrassed and angry all at the same time. I knew, however, that as long as I was president, we would never go through anything like this again. At some level, I thought this answered the question of whether my time at DMU was coming to an end. I was about to enter the last year of my contract, and I truly believed this was the answer I needed. If I could no longer grow this enterprise, my work was done.

The second thing this did for me was to begin discussions about what was next with board leadership. I recall talking with Dr. Mike Witte, who was chair of the board at the time, and I mentioned that being landlocked created a major obstacle in being able to grow the enterprise. When he asked what I thought we should do next, I told him, "If only we had more land to grow. We are in a bad spot here. We can't grow north because the campus would be divided by Grand Avenue, and to purchase property across the street, then tear it down and rebuild, would be cost prohibitive." And it was clear that there would be no option to build a skywalk over Grand Avenue. We couldn't grow west because of Wesley

Acres, an assisted living facility, and we couldn't grow east because of the church and the condominiums. The planning and zoning board had made it clear that we could not grow south because of the detention basin and the fight we could not win with the neighbors.

After regrouping for a few days after the planning and zoning meeting, I gave my immediate past chair, Dr. Larry Baker, a call to test an idea. He, too, asked what I thought we should do, and I said that the university needed more land because we will never be able to grow here. I also indicated that I would be glad to identify land that would allow future administrations to expand the campus, but until that happened, DMU needed to give up on the idea of being able to do anything more. I talked about the success of Purple and Proud as my final act in demonstrating that we could raise $25 million.

Although I was proud of the accomplishments I had made, deep down I truly believed it was time to move on. I was afraid, however, that my idea of succession planning would not work well as, again, I became aware of the consternation on campus about the role of the provost. The person hired in the role was perceived to be working against me, not working with me. All my efforts to build and foster a collaborative work environment were being challenged. My board reassured me that if anything were to happen to me or if I chose to move on, they would decide upon the interim plan and would not need to follow any prescribed succession plan anyway. I took comfort from knowing that an external interim leader would be selected, not the person perceived to be my heir apparent on campus.

At some level, this gave me a sense of calm that I could move on with peace of mind. Yet when Dr. Baker asked me more intently about this idea of needing more space, I said, "Dr. Baker, we need to at least double our acreage, perhaps to about forty acres of land, to really allow this place to grow. There were no such plots of land in ideal locations within the city limits, but perhaps we could look to buy land for expansion, and I would consider that a gift to the next administration." He jokingly said, "We've been trying to figure out how to keep you. If we need to buy more land for expansion, why not do just that?" I laughed and said, "Wait, what? You think the board would allow me to relocate the campus?"

His answer was, "I would not be opposed to that idea. Give the other members of the executive committee a call to see what they think."

From that day forward, I began making discreet calls to a few board members, and they were all so supportive that Mark Peiffer, my CFO, and I immediately began to look for land. Our attorney, Bill Lillis, was overjoyed and said he would help us look for land as he had represented several organizations as a real estate attorney. It was an easy decision to forgo any further deliberations with the City of Des Moines over the zoning issue. Instead, the zoning controversy gave us the shot in the arm we needed to make the right long-term decision for the university.

Within a few weeks of looking, Bill Lillis talked with one of his clients, Wayne McKinney of McKinney Family Farms, about the many acres of land his family owned in West Des Moines. Within a few days, Mark Peiffer and I were sitting in Wayne McKinney's office with his siblings to share our vision for a new campus for DMU. I recall sitting in awe as Wayne McKinney listened intently to our vision, then said, "I believe it would be iconic if Des Moines University would build on land that my family has owned." A few days later, my CFO and I signed a letter of intent to purchase eighty-eight acres of farmland from the McKinneys. In the March 2019 board meeting, I received a green light to move forward.

Once the decision was made to purchase eighty-eight acres of land, we began the work of planning for a new campus. RDG Planning and Design was selected through a competitive process to become our design team. In early meetings with the firm's leadership team, I asked, "So, just how long does it take to build an entirely new campus?" The answer was, "We can go as fast as you want us to go. It depends on how fast you want to move."

These first meetings were in the spring of 2019, and I remember sheepishly throwing out the year 2023 as a "what if." What if we completed our new campus in the 125th year of the founding of the university? That would mean building the campus and relocating within a four-year period. To my surprise, the answer was, "We can move that fast if you all do the work and move that fast!" It was a challenge, but it gave us the determination to meet that goal of completing the campus in a milestone year of celebration.

Forming a steering committee came next, and we began the work of thinking through all aspects of the needs for a new campus. We wanted it to be innovative, sustainable, state of the art, and able to adapt to changes over time. We wanted to build the campus of the future for health sciences education with a genuine desire to have it evolve over the years to stay current.

Individuals serving on the steering committee and meeting regularly with the design team were me, the CFO, the accounting business analyst/coordinator, the director of facilities, and the vice president for advancement. We visited other health sciences universities designed by RDG and brought along faculty and staff to help us consider the design, learning studios, and furnishings of these universities. We had several open forums to share details and design ideas, and we assembled groups of experts in the subjects that reflected our various areas of priority in the design of the new space.

We created built-to-scale offices on campus to allow faculty and staff to see the actual layout and design of the workspaces. Executive Leadership Team members conducted tours for faculty, staff, and students to allow the campus community to experience the various phases of the construction process. In the summer of 2022, the beam-signing ceremony was also a fun event that gave everyone in the campus community the chance to leave their mark in the heart of the new campus. During the pandemic, we never stopped planning; we just shifted to an online format.

In 2023, as we celebrated the 125th year of the founding of this university, we moved to our new campus at 8025 Grand Avenue in West Des Moines. We cleared the land, designed an innovative campus for the future, and have now built a new health sciences university from the ground up!

The decision to relocate was the right thing at the right time. It was a time when we, as a university community, had united with shared goals and a culture of respect. This bold new idea came with a degree of anxiety, of course, but it also gave us a degree of excitement that permeated the soul of the place. We took considerable pride in doing something BIG for DMU, and everyone who joined us felt the vibe.

In my September 2011 inaugural address (included in the appendix), I spoke of a future state for Des Moines University, setting aspirational and audacious goals by dreaming big. If you were to read this address today, you might wonder whether I was speaking of building an innovative campus from the ground up. Much as I would like to take credit for it, I could not have imagined this new campus in our future. Again, however, perhaps it was ordained—part of this divine master plan for both me and DMU.

CHAPTER 12

LEADERSHIP FROM THE GROUND UP: WORKING AS A TEAM

According to recent data from the American Council on Education, the average length of service for a university or college president and CEO is six years. As I write this, on the verge of my thirteenth year as president and CEO of Des Moines University, I want to look back on my experiences to determine the teachable moments that define my longevity in the role. I often explain that I never imagined remaining here for so long, but this longevity simply reflects the fact that the role continues to feel new and fresh and forever evolving.

Presidents often bail out too soon or jump to grab the next shiny object, lacking foresight about the value of the long game. At several points along the way, I considered other job prospects, yet each time there was a "next thing" to keep me engaged at DMU. In 2020, with my contract ending after nine years, I had every intention of pursuing other opportunities, particularly because I felt constrained by the limitations of our landlocked urban campus. I was the classic example of an individual who needed to move out in order to move up. Obviously, I changed my mind!

I have been working to achieve a desired end state for my Executive Leadership Team since I arrived at DMU. Over the years, we have had multiple configurations as members of the team came and went and took on new roles and responsibilities. As we evolved as a team, what was most important to me was to ensure that we had a basic understanding of who we are and why we exist. We created an ELT covenant in those early years and committed to five basic guiding principles: respect team members, accept responsibility, communicate, collaborate, and be visionary (see the appendix). It's a work in progress, but my team members are truly becoming enthusiastic ambassadors for each other.

The Executive Leadership Team meets weekly, and I also have monthly or biweekly one-on-one meetings with each of them. Subsets meet as projects may require. An admissions recruitment issue may bring together the deans along with the vice president for advancement, the vice president of academic and student affairs, and our chief diversity officer. They are the responsible leaders who make sure that university strategy toward recruiting students covers all pertinent points.

To be a member of the team, we had to agree to be respectful of each other and work collaboratively. "Trust" is an easy word to say, but it is so hard to achieve. The phrase "trust but verify" is closer to everyone's reality. Sometimes, however, verifying something takes way too long. We often find ourselves doubting, questioning, and speaking against members of the team because we truly are not able to verify that they accept full responsibility for their roles.

Most of the conflicts within the team, especially in my early years, boiled down to perceptions that someone was not stepping up to lead, not being responsible for his or her area, or somehow slacking off because things were not moving as quickly as others might want. There was a time when the derogatory phrase "weak link" was used to describe certain members of the team.

My role has often been that of ringleader, arbitrator, referee, and coach. I sometimes find myself echoing Rodney King: "Can we all just get along?" Some of the simplest things can become major challenges if people choose to avoid sharing and caring. I am a firm believer that if we take the time to get to know people, build relationships with them, and come to see them as colleagues, not enemies, we can find a way to be productive together. It takes courage. It takes openness. And it takes honesty. It can be hard to call out a problem, address it head-on, accept responsibility for it, and be big and bold enough to admit that you are wrong. A simple apology can go a long way.

I consider my approach to leadership somewhat of an anomaly. Although it has been proudly described as a flat organizational structure by design, which allows for a collaborative team approach, it means that I have far more direct reports than most presidents—fourteen individuals began reporting to me after the role of provost was removed in 2021. Every leader has a direct line to me as president, which causes some to wonder whether I am micromanaging. Actually, I have been approached by accreditation review teams that seem curious to learn more about this structure.

What many fail to see is the empowerment that comes from giving all members of this team the ability to own their responsibilities and own their place on the team. There are so many examples of how this approach facilitates collaborative efforts without extra layers of authority. What has been bypassed is the often unnecessary task of having an idea vetted by someone else before it is decided upon. The way we function allows us to vet ideas with the comfort of knowing that trusted colleagues are all on the same team and all want the same outcome. Ideas can be vetted, consensus gained, and projects executed—all within the space of a few conversations.

The evolution of this flat structure, of having so many people reporting to me directly, comes from my experiences as a new president not knowing whom to trust. Wanting to be a more engaged and active president, I felt the need to get to know everyone and to invite everyone to get to know me. That allowed people to become more comfortable bringing ideas to me directly. There was an expediency that came with that. We could get to consensus sooner and make decisions more efficiently. Removing the layers allowed ideas to flourish and trust to be built.

Although I wonder sometimes if my philosophy is really working, I'm determined to prove that a structure that first acknowledges the value we place on the relationships we build with each other will outshine any other variable of institutional effectiveness. Key roles and responsibilities carefully articulated in position descriptions will attract the right talent. Minimum responsibilities and expected skill sets are typically outlined in position descriptions, and most of us will not hire someone without making sure that they meet these minimum standards. Therefore, anyone hired in a leadership position should have the basic ability to perform the role.

What makes the difference, however, is the personality, style of engagement, and culture of the organization. There are too many examples of good people who have failed in their leadership roles. Often, they could function perfectly well, but other variables got in their way. I look at my leadership team knowing that all of them are qualified to do their jobs. That's a given. What matters most is knowing that the environment we create fosters a sense of community and well-being that defines just how effectively and successfully the team will perform.

At times, however, despite my constant efforts and my sense of personal worth and achievement, I find myself growing weary in my theory. Then I remind myself that there is a power much greater than me, that God is in control. This strengthens my faith and gives me the confidence to lean on him as I live my life—always prayerful and always grateful for the opportunity.

CHAPTER 13

LIVING THE DOUBLE STANDARD: STEREOTYPES, JUDGMENTS, AND FIRST IMPRESSIONS

There have been times when I have had to acknowledge the ways in which I believe I have been treated differently as a president and CEO than a man would have been treated. Race and gender matter in the perceptions and realities of leadership, and I have experienced firsthand this double standard, which leads me to believe that regardless of capability, knowledge, skill, and accomplishments, there are subtle and sometimes blatant differences in how women and men are acknowledged.

My early experiences at DMU were clearly different because I was often asked whether I really understood the place well enough to decide how to make changes. My background and success in similar organizations were not enough. Yet previous leaders with fewer credentials or less credibility were given the benefit of the doubt. Asking whether I had a dog became code for "we don't know enough about her." A tendency to expect a female leader to share more and reveal more about her family, personal ideations, or hobbies seemed logical to most, yet few would expect this of a male leader in his early years of engagement.

The harshness of the tone of debate and confrontation also appeared to be different. There was no filter in the boldness of inquiries when dealing with me, whereas similar inquiries directed toward male leaders were soft-pedaled, perhaps out of fear of retribution. In my early days at DMU, especially following major personnel decisions, it became fair game in open forums to expect me to explain my rationale for making leadership decisions.

Spinning a negative story about a female leader seems easy, while there is a reluctance to do the same for a male leader. Those who intended to expose what they considered to be my failed leadership leaked many stories of chaos on campus to the press. Inquiries from the media to see if there was a story to share were common. When I accepted one of those inquiries from local media, I invited the chairman of our board of trustees to join me.

The questioning centered around the rumors of mass departures of our faculty, our failure to successfully raise funds for the organization, and our declining enrollment. Every point was disputed with the facts to validate our reality. Thanks to my chairman of the board, the truth was shared with a positive endorsement of the board's support of my vision for transforming the university. My chairman then asked, "Can you write the story of the accomplishments of our new president in her first few years on the job?" There was silence. And, of course, that story was never written.

Mean girl behavior—women treating women badly—is also a sign of this double standard. Rarely do you find a group of men plotting to undermine a male colleague. They either quietly support him or step aside to allow him to move up the ladder with a hope that when it's their time, he will return the favor. Women, on the other hand, may be more critical, questioning, and doubtful of themselves and, therefore, more reluctant to support their female colleagues.

I recall being questioned by a few of my female colleagues about my desire to become a college president. One said, "Why aren't you satisfied where you are? You're making a major contribution at this level, so why are you still pursuing something else?" Instead of encouragement and understanding, there was a perceived doubt of my ability to go to the next level or a perceived desire to see me remain at the same level with them. This also plays out in many encounters with women, who first size you up to determine where you stand in relation to them. Judgments are made based on your appearance, sometimes superficially, and often with a reluctance to try to first get to know you.

The evidence of this comes when I talk with someone after the first, second, or third time of encountering them and having them say, "You are not what I thought you would be!" My best example of this comes from the long-standing relationship I have with my executive assistant, Christina Henderson. She interviewed for the job of being my executive assistant when I served as provost and executive vice president at Meharry Medical College. She had an accomplished record of supporting other administrative officers in a neighboring academic institution. I thought she presented well, and I was eager to have a second conversation with her.

When offered the position, Christina accepted, and she began her journey with me in the fall of 2007. After a few months of great conversations, of building rapport, she admitted that she had initially thought I would be serious and no-nonsense in my interactions with her. She went on to say that, based on her first impression, she could not have predicted the lighthearted encounters we were having. Lesson learned: my professional demeanor in a job interview was perceived to be so formal that my authentic self came as a surprise.

This wasn't the first time that people have misread me, basing their impressions on little other than my external appearance and sometimes quiet demeanor. I have now come to embrace this as an asset, and I find myself enjoying their surprise when people learn that I'm really an okay person. Why should this matter? Because many of us spend too much time worrying about how others perceive us. Instead, I have chosen to remain comfortable being my authentic self, being comfortable in my own skin, and to allow those who are equally comfortable with that dynamic to get to know me at their own pace.

CHAPTER 14

WORLD CONDITIONS AND RESPECT FOR EVERYONE: PERSONAL AND ORGANIZATIONAL TRANSITIONS

My philosophy of leadership centers around the basic premise of the Golden Rule: treat everyone the way that you want to be treated. Additionally, the principles of servant leadership, of serving instead of being served, define the style that I brought to my role at Des Moines University. I have described a flat organizational structure, which by design allows for the relationships among team members to flourish as we focus on the common thread that connects us, that is, as we work together to realize our collective vision and the ultimate positive advancement of our organization.

Every organization has its own culture, and at DMU we work hard to follow the basic guiding principles of accountability, collaboration, honesty, inclusiveness, and wellness. This is enhanced by what I expect of my Executive Leadership Team: acknowledge these core values and the importance of the relationships we build within the team. Everyone has a role to play. We are not all good at everything, but we optimize our impact by relying on the strengths of each member, which minimizes the weaknesses. We strive for excellence in all that we do, and we operate as ONE. It is not about the individual but about the team, and in the broadest sense the team encompasses the entire organization. And in all that we do, we take the time to recognize efforts and show people how much we appreciate what they do.

We have now relocated to our new campus, which was a major transition for the university. COVID-19 had a huge impact as we worked collaboratively to stay true to our mission and prepare our students for their careers in the health sciences, even when we needed to rethink the delivery of our curriculum and the services we could provide in person. The lingering traces of COVID-19, as well as the transformative opportunity to relocate an entire campus, have had effects that truly were out of our control.

Unfortunately, the world around us continues to churn and burn with divisive politics, global unrest, and terrorist attacks. Although we work hard to maintain a stable work environment with collaborative endeavors that support and respect everyone, we are not always mindful of the personal challenges that each individual may experience.

Everyone on our Executive Leadership Team agreed to read a book by William Bridges, *Transitions: Making Sense of Life's Changes*, about the importance of recognizing the impact of individual transitions on an organization as it, too, transitions. Each individual has their own set of circumstances in life that affect them and their approach to their roles in the organization. As an organization transitions, it is important to recognize the effect of these individual transitions on the progress made within the organization. And it is important to be alert to the fact that because we all experience our external environments differently, the organization is just one cog in the wheel of our overall universe.

Similar to such traumas as homelessness, food insecurity, and domestic violence that we psychologists call adverse childhood experiences—which can undermine children's health and well-being throughout their lives—I believe that adults also bring with them into their work environments their varying reactions to personal and world conditions and that these reactions shape and define how they move forward. The more life transitions an individual has, the more these may negatively affect their day-to-day operations or the ways in which they perceive their life circumstances. Examples of these transitions could be the loss of a job, a new job with greater demands, health challenges, the stresses of parenting, the loss of a loved one, financial strain, food insecurity, racism, and microaggressions.

As leaders we cannot just focus on the transitions of the organization, we must also be mindful that the individuals within them are themselves transitioning. And depending on the number and severity of their personal circumstances, some employees will succeed with the right supportive structure, and some will fail to thrive because their environment is just too overwhelming. Awareness of and respect for the difference in employees' responses to their own transitions are important both to their well-being and to a healthy work environment.

Bridges describes each individual spinning on their own personal axis as the world around them spins at a slower or faster pace. It is important to remain mindful of this in the same way that we have come to know that personality styles directly affect the ways that people are perceived in their work environments—certain personality styles may aid or detract from team dynamics.

Personalities matter, and respect for individuals spinning on their own axis at their own pace also matters. A transformative leader must acknowledge it all.

EPILOGUE

LIVING THE DREAM

I am often asked about the approach I have taken in leading my organization. I have intentionally focused on creating an environment in which all are empowered to do their jobs. This did not happen right away. Frankly, it has taken my first thirteen years at DMU to build a culture in which people feel respected and trust my leadership. Many leaders leave too soon to feel the benefits of this evolution.

I have also been asked about my leadership style. My basic premise clearly falls within a servant leadership approach; however, I would offer that it is much more than that. I believe that I have been led to the college presidency, that I have been called to serve, not to be served. My personality lends itself to prioritizing the relationships I have with others—to valuing the power of the connections that develop when you start from a place of respect and sincerity.

I am also asked how I was able to relocate an entire campus while maintaining strong positive relationships with everyone—where did I find the courage to fulfill this audacious goal? In 2022, while we were planning for the move to the new campus, with all the many worries about whether people would feel included and would be excited, ModernThink recognized DMU as a Great College to Work For. We received honor roll status! There was a marked difference between this survey and my first Great Colleges to Work For survey in 2013, when I held my breath and hoped for the best possible results. Achievements like these give me the courage to continue.

Are we done transforming? No, we have so much more to do! We will continue to surprise everyone with the boldness of the next chapter in our story, which is taking shape even as I write this final chapter in the story of my first thirteen years as DMU's president and CEO.

Divine intervention. Manifesting what has been ordained. When I let go, let God, to follow a calling to the presidency at Des Moines University, he shielded me. He made sure that no weapon formed against me would prosper, and he covered me with body armor that could not be penetrated. My faith grew as I remained calm and prayerful, asking for guidance to do the right things for the right reasons.

Through it all, I have been able to reap the benefits of a board of trustees whose members truly believed in me and my vision for the university. As fate would have it, we are now pursuing another transformative opportunity to position this organization for the future in a manner that no one could ever have imagined. "Dreaming big" is still my rallying cry. We are living the dream even as it continues to evolve. Stay tuned for our next transformation!

APPENDIX 1

2011 INAUGURAL ADDRESS

Thank you, Dr. Grekin and Dr. Baker! Other esteemed members of the board of trustees; distinguished members of the platform participating in the ceremony; members of my honorary inaugural steering committee; my colleagues in the academy, i.e., the delegates representing colleges, universities, and associations around the country; faculty; students; alumni; staff; family; and friends. I am so pleased and proud to accept the challenge to serve as the 15th president of Des Moines University and I am honored and privileged to gather with you on this very exciting and special day.

I accept the medallion and the articles of incorporation as symbols of the leadership of this institution, and I accept the calls to service and the charges of the students, the faculty, the administration, and the alumni in the expectations you have for me in lifting this institution up to the next level. The artifacts presented by our deans, reflecting our beginnings, will be treasured and protected. As I listened and reflected on the many words of encouragement and the excitement conveyed, I am confident that we, together, can achieve and continue to strive for excellence in all that we do. We will continue to boast of our record of academic excellence and a track record of providing compassionate and patient-centered professionals for this region, this country, and the world.

I would also like to extend my deepest gratitude and appreciation to my family for traveling alongside me on this journey. My husband, Thad, and my sons Wesley, Grant, and Jordan have been a constant source of pride and support, many times making their own personal sacrifices and adjustments for the good of the entire family, and I thank you for that. We made a family commitment and I am pleased that we are now all here together. And, as you know, we traveled a long distance to get here. My hometown of McCormick, South Carolina, is some 1,100 miles away. Of course, there were a few stops along the way; four years in Greenville, South Carolina, at Furman University; twenty years in Atlanta at Emory University and Morehouse School of Medicine; and four years in Nashville at Meharry Medical College. But my roots were firmly planted in a little town in South Carolina. My parents, Hervey Wesley Walker Jr. and Leola Grant Walker, still live in McCormick and are here with me today. My sister, Dr. Maria Walker Thompson, and her family are here with me from Atlanta. Of course, there are so many other family and friends who have made this journey with me, some here today in person and others sending well wishes in spirit, and I am so pleased.

Those who have known me for a while know that I have often talked about the fact that I tend to "gather people along the way" as I journey through life, and I have made lifelong friendships. There is a phrase that "it takes a village" … to raise a child … and sometimes it appears as if I have formed a village of friends, well-wishers, mentors, and supporters along the way. Perhaps it resonates from the early teachings of my parents of adhering to the principles of the Golden Rule. I have come to know and value the intrinsic power of this very simple message as I first think of how I would like to be treated as I engage with others. So I thank my friends and colleagues from my alma mater, Furman University; from my graduate school, Emory University; from my first place of employment, Morehouse School of Medicine, where I lived for twenty years; and Meharry Medical College. The relationships I established and the friendships I will always cherish, and I thank each of you for making this journey with me.

I must also take a few minutes to acknowledge my new community here in Des Moines, Iowa. As a southerner, you grow up hearing of the virtues of southern hospitality. I must admit that midwestern hospitality is equally strong and positive, and my family and I have been impressed with the considerable outpouring of support from this community. I have again begun the process of acquiring new friends here in this great city, from Governor Terry Branstad, the immediate past president of Des Moines University, who is traveling internationally; Mayor Frank Cownie, who has welcomed me into the city; colleagues in other institutions of higher education; businesses; social and civic clubs; churches; and various other associations. I thank you for the warm welcome and look forward to partnering with you on many initiatives for the good of this community.

The words of welcome and support give me considerable personal satisfaction, because this has been quite a personal and professional journey for me to this place. However, the focus of today should not be on any one individual. The leaders of the past will number fifteen as of this day; however, there is so much more that defines this institution and its greatness and hope for the future. I stand upon the shoulders of the leaders of the past but also acknowledge the commitment of those toiling in the trenches who helped define who we are. The committed faculty and the dedicated staff over the years have stood up when they sometimes felt like falling down to ensure that we were forever mindful of the fact that our reason for being was for the students, the trainees who will go out to be of service.

As I have said from the very beginning, this day is not so much about me, but about this great institution, Des Moines University. So today, we celebrate an institution. We gather to rejoice in the university's history, its traditions, its successes, and its rich potential.

So where did all this begin?

Des Moines University has evolved from its very modest yet noble founding in 1898 by Summerfield Saunders Still, nephew of the founder of osteopathy, Andrew Taylor Still, and his wife, Ella Daugherty Still. We began as the Summerfield Saunders (S.S.) Still College of Osteopathy, and over this period of 113 years we have undergone several name changes and locations. What has been preserved, however, are the spirit and tenacity of our founding fathers and mothers who were forever striving for validation and excellence in the delivery of care. We have had a long and distinguished history. We are:

1. One of the first osteopathic institutions to offer a diploma rather than a certificate to its graduates

2. Among the first to lead osteopathic education to adopt a four-year program of professional studies

3. The first college of osteopathic medicine and surgery to be accepted into membership into the Association of Academic Health Centers

4. The first health sciences university to be born out of an osteopathic college

5. The first osteopathic medical school to begin a physician assistant program

6. The first College of Podiatric Medicine and Surgery established in a health sciences university

There were many early accomplishments, and this institution has persevered sometimes in spite of its many challenges. This very point was acknowledged in the address President Leonard Azneer, our eleventh president, made in 1983 at the first Founders Day program: "There were dark days when many believed that this institution could not survive even as a college of osteopathic medicine. Its demise was foretold and the obituary had already been written when, like a phoenix rising almost from the ashes, the future of this institution began to unfold anew. This time it was painted in the bold strokes of hope and courage, of faith in self, and commitment to the osteopathic medical philosophy."

Although he is no longer with us, we acknowledge the contributions of President Azneer, who was described as a builder and led this institution forward in spite of the many challenges before him.

In that same Founders Day program, keynote speaker Dr. Murray Goldstein—a noted alumnus from the Class of 1950 and the first D.O. to work for the National Institutes of Health, and at the time the assistant surgeon general of the U.S. Public Health Service—also challenged this university to "decide what it will be when it grows up." He challenged us to "reach maturity … become a University of Health Sciences" and "enter the community of scholars." He challenged us in the spirit of rededication to "direct this University to being a center of academic excellence in education, in community service, and in the pursuit of new knowledge."

The challenge was addressed in the establishment of additional training programs during the 1980s to expand the health care team to include training in podiatric medicine and surgery and several programs in the College of Health Sciences—physician assistant, physical therapy, postprofessional doctor of physical therapy, public health, and health care administration.

Those statements were made in 1983 at our first Founders Day and acknowledged and reaffirmed by President Richard Ryan in our 100-year anniversary in 1998. And to the credit of President Emeritus Ryan, our health sciences university again raised the bar and realized a period of growth and stability in our academic programs, which focused on excellence and credibility. Governor Branstad continued the push forward in raising greater awareness of the university, its mission, its vision, and the impact it has had on this city, region, and the nation.

So here we are today … a health sciences university … a unique configuration of colleges and programs that now defines us. What a wonderful journey, what a wonderful track record we now enjoy. So I come to this place understanding and respecting this history, and I am mindful of the challenges, the worries, the setbacks, the revolutions, and the successes of the past. However, I intend to take the wisdom of the leaders from the past, the goodwill and personal triumphs of those who soldiered on down in the trenches, those who endured but ever focused on what could be, and I combine that with a desire and willingness to be so much better than we ever imagined before.

What an amazing transformation there has been from those early days from the Still College building at 1428 West Locust Street in downtown Des Moines to the now-sprawling 24-acre campus at 3200 Grand. There is so much we can be proud of today.

So where do we go from here?

At my first commencement this year in May, I gave a charge to the graduating class. The charge began with a favorite quote of mine, which is: "Know that you will make your living by what you get, but you will make a life by what you give." I asked that they go and serve by fulfilling the mission of this school in the delivery of medical care, in the advancement of knowledge, and in strengthening our system of health care. I asked that they reach far, dream colossal dreams, set audacious goals, be bold in leadership, and, in the name of service to mankind, be possessed of an outrageous ambition to make things better.

In a similar way that I charged the students, I would like to also give a charge to the entire campus community.

We have been very deliberate in the past few months in working together—the board of trustees, the alumni, the administrators, faculty, staff, and students—in helping to define who we are and what we hope to convey as our purpose, our core values, and our vision for the future.

So whereas we are in the midst of this process, I am asking that we, too, reach far, dream colossal dreams, and set audacious goals. Our collective vision for the future should be rich with an outrageous ambition to make things better, not just for our students, our faculty, our staff, but for the larger community. I ask that we dream big and set aspirational goals, but be forever mindful of the steps, sometimes first steps, sometimes baby steps, that we must take to move forward.

I have taken to heart the position recently offered by Steve Wartman of the Association of Academic Health Centers, who states that "health sciences universities like us should no longer be able to say that their missions are solely education, research, and service/patient care. Missions instead must be viewed as functions that enable institutions to achieve their overarching mission, which ultimately is the improved health and well-being of their communities."

In order to do this, we must be deliberate in what has been called a recalibration, a value proposition for all academic health centers.

As we look to the future, we must make sure that education is more explicitly linked to societal needs, research to health, and patient care to specific community and regional needs. We cannot do that alone without the community and the recognition of the fact that there are other members of the team who will be there with us in shaping the future of health care. Interprofessional collaborations and interprofessional training will be at the center of these new calibrations.

So what are the expectations for the future of health sciences universities like DMU?

I would offer that we be very deliberate and be bold in our vision. I believe we, too, must recalibrate. Not only does it mean a new way of thinking to embrace best practices, but also a boldness in approach, which requires that we become very deliberate in our effort to connect with the community at large.

So I can imagine a Des Moines University of the future that has become a destination institution where we will be recognized nationally for our innovative health education programs that promote lifelong learning.

We will be recognized as a leader and partner in the delivery of premier services that impact health, wellness, and education in our communities.

We will partner to engage in transforming our communities to be healthy and well.

And we will value the discovery of knowledge and cultivate distinctive faculty and student researchers with a commitment to health and excellence.

Personally, I have a passion for higher education and a commitment to academic excellence. My vision for the future of Des Moines University centers around a simple principle of EXCELLENCE.

In order to raise the bar and strive to be bold in our vision, we must never forget and be forever mindful of the fact that we are all in this together. In all that we do, we place the highest priority on respect for the dignity and diversity of the members of the entire campus community—patients, students, faculty, employees, and volunteers. We are committed to fostering a climate that doesn't just tolerate differences but treasures them, because we become better citizens of this world and better health care providers when we embrace the rich opportunities afforded to us when we learn from our differences.

I see DMU becoming a destination institution for individuals committed to learning in an environment that promotes excellence, from the delivery of the curriculum in state-of-the-art facilities and hands-on learning experiences that stress the personal touch in a compassionate and holistic manner, to a curriculum that addresses culturally competent care. And as we promote health and wellness, we embrace a philosophy which challenges us to shift from an illness model to a wellness model of care.

We cannot be excellent … we cannot be great … until we focus and prioritize our efforts.

How we get there will take additional resources, which is the focus of a concerted effort that began in conjunction with the inauguration to provide fiscally for all that we hope to become. The Educational Excellence Fund is central to this vision for the future, and I would like to publicly thank all of you who have made a commitment to join with us in this journey by lending support.

So here again I reflect on the phrase "it takes a village." Not just for raising children, but for raising up an academic health center, a health sciences university, a Des Moines University. We are all in this together, this board of trustees, the administrative staff, the faculty, the students, the alumni, the community and business leaders, and our friends and supporters.

We ARE doing a world of good.

What it means is that we will be very deliberate in our mission, we will be very intentional in our approach, and we will be committed to doing what is right with integrity and compassion, all for the good of others. And since our mission of improving lives in the global community by educating diverse groups of compassionate health professionals is at the heart and soul of who we are and our purpose, we *must* be very deliberate in charting our path for the future.

And how shall we do it?

Given our purpose, given our vision for the future, we will continue to stand on one simple principle—that is we will remain committed to health and committed to excellence in all that we do.

I accept the calls to service, and I challenge us all to move forward together in striving for excellence. And as I heed the call to service, accept the challenge for leadership, and reaffirm my own personal core values of inclusivity, diversity, integrity, compassion, and collaboration and my own commitment to integral leadership and servant leadership, then let us all go forward in celebrating Des Moines University, for all that it has been and all that it will become, for we are truly doing a world of good with a commitment to health and excellence.

APPENDIX 2

EXECUTIVE LEADERSHIP TEAM COVENANT

As professionals and members of the Executive Leadership Team at Des Moines University, we commit today to be accountable for the principles defined in this Team Covenant. These principles were developed by the team and will be mutually reinforced by the team. While incorporating core values, the statements reflect our commitment to a working relationship based on partnership, excellence, and integrity. They also reflect the expectations that others should have toward the members of this ELT.

The members of the Executive Leadership Team of Des Moines University commit to the following guiding principles:

1. Respect team members
    - Be respectful of the roles and responsibilities of each ELT member.
    - Accept and affirm the team's decisions.

- Value different ways of thinking.
- Value different disciplines within the university community.

2. Accept responsibility
   - Be accountable for my responsibilities and actions.
   - Seek to be decisive.
   - Hold others accountable.
   - Accept constructive criticism to assist in personal development.

3. Communicate
   - Communicate with honesty and clarity.
   - Practice listening skills.
   - Address concerns directly with team members.
   - Promote open discussions in ELT meetings.

4. Collaborate
   - Work as a team to achieve the strategic goals of DMU.
   - Think beyond your department, college, or discipline.
   - Seek the best interests of DMU even if it conflicts with your personal or professional interests.
   - Accept and embrace change.

5. Be visionary
   - Invest critical thought in new ideas.
   - Support and nurture new projects after a thorough review.
   - Align results with the mission of DMU.
   - Actively shape the future of Des Moines University.

www.ingramcontent.com/pod-product-compliance
Lightning Source LLC
Chambersburg PA
CBHW061801070526
44586CB00023B/2657